Antonio Gramsci and the Question of Religion

Antonio Gramsci and the Question of Religion provides a new introduction to the thought of Gramsci through the prisms of religious studies and comparative ethics. Bruce Grelle demonstrates that many of Gramsci's key ideas—on hegemony, ideology, moral reformation, "traditional" and "organic" intellectuals—were formulated with simultaneous considerations of religion and politics. Identifying Gramsci's particular brand of Marxism, Grelle offers an overview of Gramsci's approach to religion and applies it to contemporary debates over the role of religion and morality in social order and social change. This book is ideal for students and scholars interested in Gramsci, religion, and comparative ethics.

Bruce Grelle is Professor and Director of the Religion and Public Education Project in the Department of Comparative Religion and Humanities at California State University, Chico, USA.

D1521064

Antonio Gramsci and the Question of Religion

Ideology, Ethics, and Hegemony

Bruce Grelle

LONDON AND NEW YORK

First published 2017
by Routledge
2 Park Square, Milton Park, Abingdon, Oxon OX14 4RN

and by Routledge
711 Third Avenue, New York, NY 10017

Routledge is an imprint of the Taylor & Francis Group, an informa business

British Library Cataloguing-in-Publication Data
A catalogue record for this book is available from the British Library

Library of Congress Cataloging in Publication Data
Names: Grelle, Bruce, author.
Title: Antonio Gramsci and the question of religion : ideology, ethics,
and hegemony / Bruce Grelle.
Description: New York : Routledge, 2016. | Includes bibliographical
references and index.
Identifiers: LCCN 2016013411 | ISBN 9781138190641 (alk. paper)
Subjects: LCSH: Religious ethics. | Religion. | Ethics. | Gramsci,
Antonio, 1891-1937--Influence.
Classification: LCC BJ1188 .G74 2016 | DDC 195--dc23
LC record available at https://lccn.loc.gov/2016013411

ISBN: 978-1-138-19064-1 (hbk)
ISBN: 978-1-138-19065-8 (pbk)
ISBN: 978-1-315-64088-4 (ebk)

Typeset in Bembo
by Saxon Graphics Ltd, Derby

For Debbie and Emily

Contents

Acknowledgments

This book has been a long time in the making, and I have had the support of many people during that time. I take this opportunity to thank my colleagues in the Department of Comparative Religion and Humanities at California State University, Chico. I am also grateful to the College of Humanities and Fine Arts at CSU, Chico for a research grant and a sabbatical that facilitated work on this project. I thank my parents, brothers, and in-laws for their ongoing encouragement and support. Most of all, I wish to thank my wife, Debbie, and my daughter, Emily, for their love and care. Their presence always reminds me of what is most valuable in a man's life.

Quotations from *Selections from the Prison Notebooks of Antonio Gramsci* (New York: International Publishers, 1971) are printed by permission. An earlier version of chapter six appeared in *Soundings: An Interdisciplinary Journal* (78: 3/4, 1995) and is used here by permission.

Introduction

Antonio Gramsci and the Question of Religion: Ideology, Ethics, and Hegemony

A 2009 book titled *Perspectives on Gramsci* assembled a dozen scholars from the humanities and social sciences to demonstrate the contemporary importance of Gramsci to their respective fields of inquiry. According to its editor, the book "will be of interest to students and scholars of political philosophy, economics, film and media studies, sociology, education, literature, post-colonial studies, anthropology, subaltern studies, cultural studies, linguistics and international relations" (Francese 2009: i). Notably absent from this list are religious studies and comparative ethics. Indeed, these are typically not included among those fields of inquiry that have been substantially influenced by an encounter with Gramsci's thought. This is despite the fact that many of his key ideas—ideology, hegemony, common sense, "traditional" and "organic" intellectuals, passive revolution, intellectual and moral reformation—were developed in the context of his reflections on the history of religions, especially Christianity, and in the context of his interpretation of Marxism according to a religious paradigm. In the present work I explore how the study of religion and ethics can benefit from a more thorough engagement with Gramsci's thought.

A main goal of the critical study of religion and ethics is to understand the roles that religious–moral discourses play in struggles for power between competing social groups. How are religion and morality used for political purposes? What roles do religious ideas, myths, ethics, rituals, and institutions play in the creation, maintenance, and transformation of societies? What part do religion and morality play in the exercise of domination by some groups over others and also in struggles for liberation from such domination? Gramsci's writings address these questions about the politics of religion and morality in an especially insightful and suggestive manner.

It may at first seem odd to suggest that the work of Antonio Gramsci (1891–1937), a militant Marxist intellectual and one of the founders of the Italian Communist Party, might prove to be a rich resource for the study of religion. After all, Marxism is notorious for describing religion as "the opium of the people"—as nothing more than a form of "ideology" that reflects underlying social–economic factors and justifies the interests of the dominant classes in history and society. On this view, religion is seen as an illusion and as a form of false consciousness. Morality is regarded simply as a cloak for class interests and as a form of social control. However, in this book, I argue that Gramsci's reformulation of the Marxist concepts of ideology and hegemony enable us to keep questions about the politics of religion and morality in sharp focus while moving beyond the determinism and reductionism of orthodox Marxist accounts.

Gramsci defined religion as a "unity of faith between a conception of the world and a corresponding norm of conduct," but he asked why we should call this "religion" and not "ideology" or even frankly "politics"? (Gramsci 1971: 326). He drew parallels between traditional religions and modern political ideologies, and he analyzed the political role of religious and secular myths in struggles for power between competing groups. Gramsci's writings on religion move us well beyond the metaphor of religion as the "opium" of the people. He realized that religions and ethics have functioned not only as sources for the legitimation of the status quo, but also as a medium for political struggles that aim toward the transformation of society.

The first three chapters of this book provide an exposition of Gramsci's approach to what he described as "the question of religion or world-view" (Gramsci 1971: 132). Here I give an account of some of the intellectual and historical circumstances in which he developed his approach to issues of religion, ethics, ideology, and culture. I situate Gramsci's work with respect to alternative currents within Marxism and social theory and explain what it is that makes his work valuable for contemporary efforts to clarify the politics of religion and morality. In the last three chapters I appropriate some of Gramsci's key ideas and apply them to discussions in religious studies and comparative ethics. More specifically, I draw on Gramsci's thought to develop a framework for thinking about the relationship between religious ethics, social order, and social change as well as for rethinking the ideological nature of religion and morality, that is, the connection of religious–moral ideas and discourses to the interests of both dominant and oppositional social groups. Along the way I consider how Gramsci's work not only sheds light on the politics of religion and ethics, but also on the politics of the *academic study* of religion and ethics.

Gramsci's most important ideas are found in thirty-three handwritten notebooks that he kept during his long imprisonment at the hands of Italian Fascist dictator Benito Mussolini from 1926 until his release in 1937, only a few days before his death at the age of forty-six. The authoritative Italian edition of the *Prison Notebooks*—*Quaderni del carcere*—was edited by Valentino Gerratana and published by Einaudi in 1975. Columbia University Press is in the process of publishing a complete multivolume critical edition of Gramsci's *Prison Notebooks* in English, edited and translated by Joseph A. Buttigieg. As of this writing, three volumes containing notebooks one through eight have appeared in print (Gramsci 2011). I have relied primarily on *Selections from the Prison Notebooks* edited and translated by Quintin Hoare and Geoffrey Nowell Smith, which first appeared in 1971 and has since been reprinted many times (Gramsci 1971). This is still the most well-known and widely accessible edition of Gramsci's writings, and it is where many of his key ideas were first introduced to the English-speaking public. I have also drawn on several other translations and collections of Gramsci's writings and on an extensive secondary literature in English that stretches back to the 1970s, as indicated in the list of References at the end of this book.

Finally, a quick note on terminology may be in order. The difficulties involved in the interpretation of Gramsci's prison writings are widely known. The fragmentary and elliptical character of the *Prison Notebooks* and their recourse to tricks to deceive the prison censors have been noted by his translators and editors (see editors in Gramsci 1971: xiii). Where relevant, I have sought to address debates about what Gramsci may have meant by his use of certain terms in the context of the discussion at hand. As for my own terminology, I generally follow Gramsci's lead in defining "religion" as "a conception of the world and corresponding norm of conduct" (1971: 326; see also Wainwright 2010). This linkage between "conceptions" and "norms" is highlighted by my frequent if infelicitous usage of the phrase "religious–moral." When I use the term "discourse," as in the phrase "religious–moral discourse," I have in mind the ways that historically and socially situated groups of people communicate these conceptions and norms through language as spoken and written and as institutionalized in their social practices and traditions. I generally use the term "morality" to refer to people's notions of right and wrong and good and evil and to their ideas and assumptions about what kind of life is worth living. I generally use the term "ethics" to refer to the study of morality—to self-conscious reflection about morality, whether one's own or that of others, although as is the case in everyday conversation there is some slippage between these two terms and I trust the context will make my meaning clear.

This book's intended audience includes college and university students and teachers along with members of the general public who are looking for an introduction to Gramsci's thought as it bears on religion and ethics. I also hope that chapters four through six might make a modest contribution to scholarly discussions in the field of comparative religious ethics.

1 Religious Ethics, Ideology, and Culture

The British philosopher and historian of religion Ninian Smart once observed that there seems to be a natural tendency for students of religion to overly "spiritualize" their subject matter. Our attention is often drawn to such overtly "religious" topics as conversion or enlightenment experiences, exotic myths and rituals, or theories and doctrines about gods and the afterlife. This is unfortunate for religious studies because, as Smart explains,

> the process of Christianization of northern Europe [for example] is imperfectly understood unless it is clear why rulers found the new faith a useful ideology for shaping political power, and often Buddhist origins are seen independently of the socio-political changes occurring in the Gangetic region ...
>
> (Smart 1983: 273)

Following up on Smart's comments, I would add that there appears to be a corresponding tendency among students of ethics to overly "rationalize" or "philosophize" their subject matter by concentrating on such overtly "ethical" topics as the rational structure of moral argument and the justification of moral claims. This is unfortunate for the study of ethics because it obscures the nature and function of religious–moral discourses as "languages of persuasion," which, along with the threat or exercise of force and violence, are a primary means by which patterns of power, interest, and influence are either maintained or subverted, legitimated, or challenged (Bird 1981). In other words, students of religion and ethics often lose sight of politics.

In the 1970s and 1980s, as comparative religious ethics was emerging as a distinctive field of study in many colleges and universities across the United States and Canada, a number of leading scholars proposed that the field should follow the example of academic moral philosophy by concentrating its attention on the analysis of moral reasoning within and between religious traditions. While there were disputes between those working in analytic and Kantian traditions over questions of ethical theory, there was general agreement among them that the goal of comparative religious ethics should be to describe, analyze, and classify the moral systems of different religious thinkers, texts, and traditions according to the patterns of moral reasoning that they exhibit.

Other scholars advocated a more "holistic" understanding of the field. While the moral reasoning approach stresses the "autonomy of morality" and assumes that it is possible and desirable to analyze morality on its own terms, the holistic approach stresses the historicity and cultural specificity of moral claims and discourses. It seeks to identify, interpret, and appreciate the moral dimensions of larger religious and cultural systems. The focus is not so much on forms of moral reasoning as it is on forms of life, not so much on argument or justification as on ethos. While advocates of the holistic approach do not abandon inquiry into patterns of moral reasoning, they insist that such patterns cannot be adequately described or understood apart from a consideration of the broader contexts of worldview, culture, and history.[1]

From a holistic perspective, the claims and discourses of morality are intimately related to a people's *worldview* and are partially constitutive of a people's *ethos*. That is to say that moralities not only reflect a vision of the way reality is and can be; they also play a role in the creation and embodiment of the reality described by the worldview. As famously explained by anthropologist Clifford Geertz,

> A people's "ethos" is the tone, character, and quality of their life, its moral and aesthetic style and mood; it is the underlying attitude toward themselves and their world that life reflects. Their worldview is their picture of the way things in sheer actuality are, their concept of nature, of self, of society. It contains their most comprehensive ideas of order ... the ethos is made intellectually reasonable by being shown to represent a way of life implied by the actual state of affairs which the worldview describes, and the worldview is made emotionally acceptable by being presented as an image of an actual state of affairs of which such a way of life is an authentic expression.
>
> (1973: 127)

In the present work I build on the holistic view that the study of "ethics" is concerned not only with moral reasoning, but also with the full range of "normative activity that creates and sustains an ethos" (Reynolds 1979: 23). Yet it is my own position that the holistic approach has not gone far enough in the direction of a *critical* and *contextual* understanding of the aims of comparative religious ethics. While it situates the moral dimensions of a religious tradition *within* the context of that tradition considered as a whole, it has not paid sufficient attention to the interaction *between* religious and moral discourses on the one hand, and the wider contexts of society and politics on the other hand. An awareness of these broader contexts is especially important for understanding the dynamic nature of religious–moral systems, their role in processes of historical and societal change, and, more particularly, their role in struggles for power and influence between competing social groups.

What is key for understanding comparative religious ethics as a form of critical inquiry is the recognition that, as languages of persuasion, all moralities perform an *ideological* function insofar as they tend "to legitimate particular patterns of decision-making and hence particular patterns of influence and power" (Bird 1981: 165; see also Hindery 2008). As Bruce Lincoln reminds us with the fourth of his *Theses on Method*, one of the main questions that we should ask of the religious and moral discourses that we study is "Who speaks here?" That is, regardless of its putative or apparent author, what person, group, or institution is responsible for the text or discourse with which we are presented? Moreover, what audience is being addressed by the author, in what context, and through what "system of mediations"? What interests are at stake? What would be the consequences of this project of persuasion if it should happen to succeed? Who wins? Who loses? What and how much do they stand to win or lose? (Lincoln 2012: 1). The purpose of posing such questions is not to endorse the superficially critical exercise of unmasking or deconstructing the ideological uses of religions and moralities simply for the sake of unmasking. On the contrary, as Frederick Bird explains,

> To know the ways in which particular moralities serve to legitimate configurations of interest and power is neither to imply that these interests are illegitimate nor to suggest the moral aims and standards as articulated are without compelling influence of their own. Rather, reference to the ideological dimensions of moralities calls attention to the frequently unacknowledged legitimating function of moralities.
>
> (1981: 165–166)

The concept of "ideology" has had a complex and ambiguous history.[2] The origins of the term can be traced back to Antoine Destutt de Tracy (1754–1836), a French aristocrat-turned-revolutionary, who coined the term to designate a new "science of ideas" that would constitute one aspect of a more general science of the human animal conceived as a branch of zoology. The new science would set aside metaphysical and religious dogmas and prejudices in favor of investigating the origin and development of ideas, thereby contributing to the Enlightenment dream of a true and universal knowledge of human nature. Destutt de Tracy and his colleagues in the Moral and Political Sciences division of France's Institute Nationale came to be known as "ideologues," whose task it was to disseminate the French Revolution's religion of rationalism. The pejorative connotations often associated with the term have been traced to Napoleon Bonaparte. While initially pleased with the work of the Institute, as he began to renege on his revolutionary idealism Napoleon turned against the ideologues, accusing them of fanaticism and of fostering the very metaphysical abstractions and dogmas they had set out to discredit (Eagleton 2007: 67–68).

Something like the concept of ideology had been anticipated in the work of such philosophers as Machiavelli, Francis Bacon, Baron d'Holbach, and Claude Adrien Helvetius, all of whom offered some version of a materialist critique of the foundations of knowledge. Francis Bacon's investigations of the "idols" of conventional knowledge, for example, or the claim by Helvetius that "our ideas are the necessary consequences of the societies in which we live" (cited in Rudé 1980: 15), foreshadowed the preoccupations of subsequent discussions of ideology. They rest on the proposition that ideas are not autonomous, that their roots lie elsewhere, and that something central about ideas will be revealed if we can discover the nature of the relationship between ideas and the material circumstances in which they arise.

Yet it is to the writings of Marx and Engels that we must turn for an understanding of the most important contemporary usages of the concept of ideology. There are a variety of well-known texts in which Marx and Engels formulate the problem of ideology as they see it. In a classic passage from *The German Ideology*, for example, they write that:

> The production of ideas, of conceptions, of consciousness, is at first directly interwoven with the material activity and the material intercourse of men – the language of real life ... The same applies to mental production as expressed in the language of the politics, laws, morality, religions, metaphysics, etc., of a people. Men are the producers of their conceptions, ideas, etc., that is, real, active men, as they are conditioned by a definite development of their productive forces and of the intercourse corresponding to these ... Consciousness can never be anything else than conscious being, and the being of men is their actual life-process ... *Morality, religion, metaphysics, and all the rest of ideology as well as the forms of consciousness corresponding to these, thus no longer retain the semblance of independence.* They have no history, no development; but men, developing their material production and their material intercourse, alter, along with this their actual world, also their thinking and the products of their thinking. *It is not consciousness that determines life, but life that determines consciousness.*
>
> (Marx and Engels 1976: 36–37, emphasis added)

For Marx and Engels, it is not enough simply to accept the vague notion that our material and social circumstances shape the way we think. Rather, what is crucial to the determination of human beliefs is not only social being or the material conditions of human existence as such, but a specific element of our circumstances, namely, the mode of production of material life. It is humanity's involvement in a particular way of producing goods and services, along with the characteristic set of social class and property relationships and technologies entailed by this mode of production, that provides the key for understanding the connection between social being and consciousness.

In a famous passage from the Preface to *A Contribution to the Critique of Political Economy*, Marx seeks to drive home this point with an architectural metaphor that has become central to subsequent discussions of ideology.

> In the social production of their life, men enter into definite relations that are indispensable and independent of their will, relations of production which correspond to a definite stage of development of their material productive forces. The sum total of these relations of production constitutes the economic *structure* of society, the real *foundation*, on which rises a legal and political *superstructure* and to which correspond definite forms of social consciousness. The mode of production of material life conditions the social, political, and intellectual life process in general. It is not the consciousness of men that determines their being, but, on the contrary, their social being that determines their consciousness.
>
> (Marx and Engels 1968: 182, emphasis added)

As we will see in the next chapter, this figure of speech has been the source of much confusion and controversy about exactly how to interpret the relationship between the economic structure of a society (the foundation or base) on the one hand and forms of religious and moral consciousness, law, and politics (the superstructure) on the other hand.

Along with this focus on the relationship between ideas and the material conditions of human existence, the Marxist concept of ideology also stresses the connection between ideology and the *interests* of social groups, and it claims that ideology, especially religion and morality, plays an important role in the exercise of class domination. These insights were crystallized by Marx and Engels in the *Manifesto of the Communist Party* when they wrote that "The ruling ideas of each age have ever been the ideas of its ruling class" (1968: 51) and by Marx in the Introduction to *Contribution to the Critique of Hegel's Philosophy of Law*, where he penned his famous assertion that "Religion is the sigh of the oppressed creature, the heart of a heartless world, just as it is the spirit of a spiritless condition. It is the *opium* of the people" (1975: 175, emphasis in original).[3]

As these and other texts make evident, the question of ideology figured prominently in the writings of Marx and Engels, yet, considering their impact on subsequent discussions of the topic, their own treatments of the topic are often ambiguous and surprisingly underdeveloped. Indeed, as historian George Rudé has noted, it is actually misleading to talk about Marx's *theory* of ideology, because the notion is nowhere so comprehensively formulated in Marx's own writings (Rudé 1980: 16). Moreover, the formulas usually associated with Marx's "theory" of ideology—"social being determines consciousness" and "base determines superstructure"— have led to divergent and sometimes contradictory understandings of the concept (Eagleton 2007: 72–84; Giddens 1979: 165–197; Larrain 1979: 35–67; McLellan 1995: 19–30).

As we will see in more detail in chapter two, this ambiguity has been a source of fundamental differences within the Marxian tradition. One current within Marxism (often attributed, though not altogether fairly, to Engels) adopted a rather mechanical and simplistic interpretation of the base–superstructure model, which gave rise to a reflection theory of consciousness and a deterministic understanding of social change. On this view, the ideological "superstructure" (religion, philosophy, morality, law, art) was seen as little more than a reflection of underlying economic realities. Societal change was determined not by thought or action but by impersonal social, historical, and economic processes that had very little to do with human will or initiative. This became the prevailing view of what came to be known as "orthodox" or "scientific" Marxism.[4]

An alternative current of thought emerged after the First World War and was highly critical of the mechanistic determinism that characterized orthodox Marxism's approach to ideology and politics. This alternative became known variously as Western Marxism, Hegelian Marxism, Marxist Humanism, or Critical Marxism and is associated not only with the name of Antonio Gramsci, but also with such figures as Georg Lukács and Ernst Bloch along with various thinkers associated with the so-called "Frankfurt School" of critical social theory, including Max Horkheimer, Theodor Adorno, and Walter Benjamin, among others. Despite the significant differences between these writers, their work broke with many Marxist orthodoxies and exhibited a more nuanced understanding of the nature and function of ideology and the role of religion, philosophy, ethics, and art in political struggles. Gramsci's work is of particular interest when it comes to thinking about the politics of religion, ethics, and ideology.

Antonio Gramsci has been described as the "theoretician of the superstructures" because of his preoccupation with questions of culture and ideology (Texier 1979). And indeed, along with his reflections on religion and ethics, Gramsci's writings cover a very wide range of "superstructural" topics: history and politics, philosophy and education, linguistics, folklore, literary criticism, and popular culture, to name just some of the areas in which he exhibited a sustained interest. The range and depth of Gramsci's writings are all the more remarkable when the conditions under which he was working are remembered. His biographers provide moving accounts of Gramsci's turbulent life: the hardships of his childhood in Sardinia; his years in Turin as a student-activist, journalist, and as a leader of the Factory Councils movement; his role as a leader of the socialist movement, a founder of the Italian Communist Party and as a delegate to the Communist International in Moscow; his election as a deputy to the Italian parliament; his arrest by the Fascists and his long imprisonment, during which time he produced the bulk of his most significant writings while suffering from frequent bouts of ill health (Fiori 1973; Joll 1977; Santucci 2010).

However, my aim here is neither to eulogize nor to provide a full exegesis of the life and work of this Italian Communist activist and intellectual.

Rather, my aim is to identify and appropriate those aspects of Gramsci's thought that can contribute to the development of a critical–contextual approach to the comparative study of religion and ethics—an approach that addresses the political dimensions of religious–moral discourses.

As mentioned in the Introduction to this book, Gramsci exhibited a deep and abiding interest in the history of religions, especially Christianity, and in questions about the relationship between religion, ethics, and society. And there are several respects in which Gramsci's approach to what he described as "the question of religion or world-view" (Gramsci 1971: 132) converges with the holistic approach to comparative religious ethics described above. As we will see in more detail in what follows, Gramsci most generally followed the lead of the Italian neo-Hegelian philosopher Benedetto Croce in defining religion as a "conception of the world which has become a norm of life" (Gramsci 1971: 344). The correspondence between holism and Gramsci's approach is underscored by the fact that Gramsci deliberately substituted the phrase *norma di vita* for Croce's *etica* in order to emphasize the connection between ethical standards or ideals promulgated by a worldview and the more concrete and practical forms of life in which they are embodied (editors in Gramsci 1971: 344). In this connection it is also worth noting the resemblance between Gramsci's conception of religion as a unity between a worldview and a corresponding norm of life and Hegel's concept of *Sittlichkeit* or ethos—the shared perceptions, beliefs, and values embodied in community customs, laws, and institutions (Femia 1981: 257). Hegel drew a distinction between *Moralität* and *Sittlichkeit*—between abstract morality and the concrete moral life or ethos that is located in and expressed through the family and the institutions of civil society. In contrast to the Kantian formalism that has exercised such significant influence over modern ethical theory, Hegelian conceptions of ethics focus not only on abstract principles of reason and morality, but also on the concrete embodiment of moral norms in a people's lifestyle and ethos (Walsh 1969; Norman 1998: 109–127).

Yet what distinguishes Gramsci's perspective from the holistic approach to religious ethics is its persistent focus on the often indirect but crucial link between religious–moral discourses and the struggle for power in history and society. As Robert Bellah has suggested, "Gramsci's view of 'religions' is instructive because it emphasizes the element of struggle, of process, of politics" (1980: 88). Gramsci criticized treatments of religion and culture that excluded

> the moment of struggle; the moment in which the conflicting forces are formed, are assembled and take up their positions; the moment in which one ethical–political system dissolves and another is formed by fire and steel; the moment in which one system of social relations disintegrates and falls and another arises and asserts itself.
>
> (Gramsci 1971: 119, cited in Bellah 1980: 88)

Gramsci was always mindful of the blurry boundaries between religion, ethics, and politics.

> Note the problem of religion taken not in the confessional sense but in the secular sense of a unity of faith between a conception of the world and a corresponding norm of conduct. But why call this unity of faith "religion" and not "ideology," or even frankly "politics".
>
> (Gramsci 1971: 326)

For all of holism's stress on the importance of contextual understanding, attention to the political uses and ideological functions of religious and moral discourses is largely missing. This blind spot is due in large part to the conception of "culture" that is at the heart of many holistic approaches to worldview and ethos.

In his classic account of this concept, Raymond Williams showed that the traditional view of culture, with its language of cooperative shaping and common contribution, has had a tendency to obscure the extent to which cultural formations are involved in the legitimation of power and the exercise of domination (1978: 112). Williams reminds us that "culture" was initially a noun of process, as in the cultivation and tending of crops, the rearing and breeding of animals, and the active culture or cultivation of the human mind (1981: 10). In the eighteenth century "culture" became a more general designation for the "spirit" (whether ideal, religious, or national) that informed the "whole way of life" of a distinct people. This "spirit" was believed to be manifest over the whole range of human activities, but was most evident in specifically "cultural" activities such as the language, morals, and styles of art that were unique to particular peoples and nations. It was in this connection that the German Romantic philosopher Johann Gottfried Herder (1744–1803) first used the plural "cultures" in contrast to the singular term "civilization," with its characteristic Enlightenment emphases on secular and progressive human development and universal rationality. This pluralistic usage became central in the development of comparative anthropology, where it continued to designate a whole and distinctive way of life shared in common by a particular people in a specific time and place (Williams 1981: 10–11; Crehan 2002: 38–42, 66).

As we will see in what follows, Gramsci's work moves us beyond a romantic conception of culture as a seamless whole-way-of-life, which rests upon a single set of shared beliefs and values. The Gramscian concept of hegemony shifts our attention to a consideration of the extent to which cultural formations are characterized by conflicting interests and by lived patterns of domination and subordination (Williams 1978: 110).

Yet Gramsci also rejected the economic reductionism and determinism characteristic of the orthodox Marxism of his day. Michael Walzer goes too far when he claims that Gramsci's writings often "point toward the replacement of political economy with a kind of cultural anthropology" (1988: 447), because Gramsci never abandoned a focus on the deep and complex connection between culture and basic economic relationships. He always viewed culture in relation to class and class conflict. Indeed, one might even say that, for Gramsci, culture is how class is lived (Crehan 2002: 71). Yet Walzer is right that Gramsci never sees culture as a mere epiphenomenon or simple reflection of more fundamental economic relations. Ideas, beliefs, and values play a role in struggles for power between competing social groups, but the precise interplay between "cultural" and "economic" factors varies in different times and different places. The question of whether one or the other of these factors is more decisive cannot be answered in the abstract but only after careful analysis of concrete historical circumstances.[5]

We will see that Gramsci's reading of history and his analysis of contemporary political realities led him to conclude that it was a mistake to view religion and morals as tools of the ruling class alone. On the contrary, as mentioned above, he realized that religious–moral discourses have functioned not only as sources for the legitimation of the status quo, but also as a medium for political struggles that challenge and aim to change the existing social order. His more nuanced account of religion and culture seriously complicates the "religion as opium of the people" metaphor that has been central to the standard Marxist approach.

In addition to this more politically dynamic view of religion and culture, Gramsci's work also provides a more differentiated view than is typical of orthodox Marxist accounts. The analysis of ideology is not restricted to "high" culture nor to the forms of consciousness associated with the two fundamental classes in industrial society—the bourgeoisie and the proletariat. Gramsci does not neglect the "religion of the intellectuals," nor does he ignore the systems elaborated by the great philosophers, but he also insists that attention must be paid to the "religion of the people" and to the less structured forms of thought, compounded of folklore, myth, and "common sense" that circulate among the traditional classes of peasants and artisans (Rudé 1980: 9, 23; Crehan 2002: 105–119).

Along with providing this more dynamic and differentiated view of culture, Gramsci's approach exhibits one further virtue that is significant for the comparative study of religion and ethics. His broad view of religion as "a unity of faith between a conception of the world and a corresponding norm of conduct" (1971: 326) allows for a comparative approach that encompasses not only traditional "religious" worldviews, but also "secular" worldviews and ethics such as Marxism, nationalism, humanism, liberalism, environmentalism, and the like. In what follows we will see that one of the most interesting features of Gramsci's work is his interpretation of Marxism itself according to a religious paradigm. This provides a framework for his many intriguing comparisons between Marxism and Christianity and for his reflections on the tasks confronting those who would organize a movement for the "intellectual and moral reformation" of society in the modern world.

In closing, let's recall a pioneering and often cited essay by Otto Maduro (1977: 366) that sums up the main ideas that characterize Gramsci's departure from the standard Marxist account of religion.

Firstly, religion is not regarded as a mere passive effect of the social relations of production; it is an active element of social dynamics, both conditioning and conditioned by social processes.

Secondly, religion is not always a subordinate element within social processes; it may often play an important part in the origination and consolidation of a particular social structure.

Thirdly, religion is not necessarily a functional, reproductive, or conservative factor in society; it is often a main (and sometimes the only) available channel to bring about a social revolution.

Finally, the scientific study of religions requires a many-sided empirical approach whose results cannot be either substituted or anticipated by theoretical constructs.

In the following two chapters, I will provide a more detailed analysis of these ideas along with an account of the intellectual and historical contexts within which Gramsci developed his perspective on "the question of religion or worldview." This will set the stage for an assessment of the significance of these ideas for a critical–contextual approach to the comparative study of religion and ethics—an approach that seeks to address a range of questions having to do with the politics of religious and moral discourses.

Notes

1 For concise overviews of the history of comparative religious ethics as a field of study see Twiss (2005) and Bucar and Stalnaker (2012). For classic examples of the moral reasoning approach see Green (1978, 1988) and Little and Twiss (1978). For examples of the holistic approach see Lovin and Reynolds (1985).
2 See Eagleton (2007), Freeden (2003), Lease (2000), Larrain (1979, 1991), McLellan (1995), and Williams (1983: 153–157).
3 See also *The German Ideology*: "The ideas of the ruling class are in every epoch the ruling ideas: i.e., the class which is the ruling *material* force of society is at the same time its ruling *intellectual* force. The class which has the means of material production at its disposal, consequently also controls the means of mental production, so that the ideas of those who lack the means of mental production are on the whole subject to it. The ruling ideas are nothing more than the ideal expression of the dominant material relations, the dominant material relations grasped as ideas; hence of the relations which make the one class the ruling one, therefore, the ideas of its dominance ... For instance, in an age and in a country where royal power, aristocracy and bourgeoisie are contending for domination and where, therefore, domination is shared, the doctrine of the separation of powers proves to be the dominant idea and is expressed as an 'eternal law'" (Marx and Engels 1976: 59).
4 See Larrain (1991) for a concise discussion of Engels' ambiguous position with respect to the mechanistic and deterministic interpretations of the base–superstructure metaphor that began to predominate in the Marxism of the 1880s.
5 Regarding the economic component of hegemony, see Boothman (1995: li–lii), Crehan (2002: 71–72), and Thomas (2010: 95–102).

2 Antonio Gramsci and "the Question of Religion or Worldview"

Antonio Gramsci is widely viewed as one of the most original and influential Marxist thinkers of the twentieth century (Hughes 1977: 96–104; Kolakowski 2005: 963; McLellan 2007: 210). This is due in large part to his innovative way of dealing with questions of ideology and culture—questions that had constituted a notorious blind spot in the mainstream Marxist theory of his day. In order to better appreciate Gramsci's originality, and in order to begin to assess his contribution to our understanding of the politics of religion and morality, it will be helpful to situate his ideas with respect to alternative currents within Marxist theory.

The Critique of Orthodox Marxism

Gramsci was writing during the heyday of a current of thought known as "orthodox" Marxism. Such writers as Karl Kautsky (1854–1938) and Georgi Plekhanov (1856–1918) presented Marxism as a comprehensive science that had discovered the immutable laws of history according to which the development of human societies could be understood.[1] This rendition of Marxism was very much in keeping with the prestige of the natural sciences and the widespread influence of evolutionary perspectives, which characterized the intellectual life of the late nineteenth and early twentieth centuries. The Marxist theory of history was widely viewed as analogous to the theory of evolution; what Darwin had achieved for our understanding of nature, Marx had achieved for our understanding of human society.[2]

At the level of *theory*, this view resulted in a deterministic and mechanistic view of historical change in which societies evolve according to laws that operate independently of human will and initiative. Religion, morality, philosophy, art, law, and politics were regarded as ephemeral superstructural reflections of underlying economic realities. This severely limited, when it did not altogether deny, the efficacy of ideas and values in the unfolding historical process.

At the level of *practice*, this Marxist orthodoxy was characterized by a fatalistic attitude that resulted in political passivity and inaction. Its predictions regarding the inevitable breakdown of capitalism and its faith in the objective necessity of a socialist future worked to undercut the urgency of any particular political program. This helps to account for the striking gap between orthodox Marxism's revolutionary rhetoric and its mildly reformist policies and actions. The responsibility for the political, intellectual, and moral character of society and the initiative for change had been shifted away from self-conscious human beings and toward abstract structural entities and impersonal forces. Marxist theory had largely ceased being understood as a guide for action and had become a scholastic exercise remote from concrete political practice.

But historical developments failed to conform to what had been predicted. The first socialist revolution occurred not in the industrialized West but in the backwater of agrarian and peasant Russia. Meanwhile, in Western Europe, where the "objective conditions" were supposedly ripe for revolution, the revolutionary workers' movement suffered monumental setbacks. With the unpredicted rise of Nazism in Germany and Fascism in Italy and Spain, it became increasingly apparent that the doctrines of orthodox Marxism were an inadequate basis upon which to understand historical developments. The need to overcome the theoretical and practical limitations of orthodox Marxism, and, more specifically, the need to rethink the role of ideology and politics in the struggle for social change became increasingly apparent. It is this realization that accounts in large part for the reorientation of Marxist theory that one finds in the work of such otherwise diverse writers as V. I. Lenin, Georg Lukács, Georges Sorel, and Antonio Gramsci.

Although Leninism would itself ultimately become a canon and arbiter of a new sort of "orthodoxy," it initially represented one major alternative to the orthodox Marxism that had been dominant throughout much of the European workers' movement prior to the First World War. Lenin had argued that belief in an inevitable capitalist crash and the passive political strategy that accompanied this belief would simply perpetuate the stability of the capitalist system. As capitalism moved into its imperialistic phase, it developed the capacity to subdue domestic class conflict and to gradually absorb societal contradictions in the metropolitan centers by displacing them to the periphery of the world system. This required a shift in focus to the "weakest links" in the world capitalist system—the underdeveloped and semi-colonial regions where the indigenous bourgeoisie was weak but where there was enough industrialization to create a class-conscious proletariat. Lenin insisted that an organized proletariat and peasantry, under the leadership of a highly disciplined revolutionary party, could accelerate the catastrophe of capitalism. Russia was the paradigmatic case.

Like Lenin, Gramsci disavowed orthodox Marxism's "economism" and determinism—its separation of economic from political struggles and its conviction that change is driven by objective laws of historical development similar in kind to natural laws (Bottomore 1991). Gramsci insisted that the distinctive contribution of Marxism is not its scientific discovery and analysis of the laws of history, but rather its emphasis upon humanity's self-creation through praxis. In conscious opposition to the positivism of orthodox Marxism, Gramsci seized upon the humanistic elements in the writings of Marx. For Gramsci, "Marx is the creator of a *Weltanschauung*" (1971: 381), and Marxism is the "philosophy of praxis." Thus, Gramsci joined with Lenin in asserting the primacy of the will, of politics, of self-conscious action (praxis).

What is important to notice at this point, however, are the very different ways in which Lenin and Gramsci understood the nature and goals of the political struggle. For while Gramsci did not believe that revolution would be the automatic outcome of the economic contradictions of capitalism, neither did he believe that the revolutionary experience of Russia could be repeated in the West. For Lenin, political struggle consisted primarily in an assault upon the state. The goal was a revolutionary seizure of state power by a tightly knit, highly organized, and disciplined political party and the establishment of a "dictatorship of the proletariat."

Gramsci shared Lenin's view regarding the importance of political struggle, but his analysis of conditions in Western Europe and the United States led him to the conclusion that the insurrectionist approach that had succeeded in Russia was unsuited for the West. The Leninist strategy was inappropriate because it failed to appreciate the extent to which the regimes of the West were based upon *consent* rather than upon the coercive violence of the state; not, to be sure, the free and rational consent posited by the social contract theorists of liberalism, but a consent rooted in what passed for common sense and in plain inertia. Such consent was secured not primarily through the power of the state, but rather through the diffusion and popularization of the worldview and morality of the bourgeoisie in the institutions of civil society. It was in connection with this effort to understand the relationship between coercion and consent and to discern how the circumstances faced by revolutionaries in the West differed from those faced by the Bolsheviks that Gramsci developed his distinctive understanding of the concept of hegemony.[3]

The Concept of Hegemony

According to Gramsci, the supremacy of a class is exercised and maintained not only through domination or rule, which is realized through the coercive organs of the state and the control of such repressive instruments as the police and the military. Rather, such supremacy is also and more commonly manifest as intellectual and moral "direction" or leadership. Within the modern societies of the West, such intellectual and moral leadership is objectified in and exercised through the institutions of civil society—the ensemble of educational, religious, and civic organizations, political parties, unions, clubs, and voluntary cultural associations.[4]

The achievement and maintenance of hegemony is largely a matter of education: "Every relationship of 'hegemony' is necessarily an educational relationship" (Gramsci 1971: 350). In this connection Gramsci speaks of the "positive educative function" of schools and churches and the "repressive and negative educative function" of the courts (Gramsci 1971: 258). Through its occupation of the institutions of civil society, the dominant group's (or coalition's) "view of reality" informs all tastes, morality, customs, religions, political and legal principles, and all social relations particularly in their intellectual and moral connotations (Femia 1975: 30–31). It comes to constitute the "common sense" of the majority of the population—"The conception of the world absorbed uncritically from the various social and cultural environments in which the moral individuality of the average man develops" (Gramsci cited in Counihan 1986: 5; see Gramsci 1971: 323, 326, 421ff.).

By way of summary, Raymond Williams provides an admirable distillation of the concept of hegemony.

> Hegemony is then not only the articulate upper level of "ideology," nor are its forms of control only those ordinarily seen as "manipulation" or "indoctrination." It is a whole body of practices and expectations, over the whole of living: our senses and assignments of energy, our shaping perceptions of ourselves and our world. It is a lived system of meanings and values—constitutive and constituting—which as they are experienced as practices appear as reciprocally confirming. It thus constitutes a sense of reality for most people in the society, a sense of absolute because experienced reality beyond which it is very difficult for most members of the society to move, in most areas of their lives. It is, that is to say, in the strongest sense a "culture," but a culture which has also to be seen as the lived dominance and subordination of particular classes.
>
> (Williams 1978: 110)

Thus, while the focus of Leninism was upon the military conquest of the state, Gramsci shifted attention to the importance of ideological and "ethical–political" struggle in what was bound to be a long and complex revolutionary process.

According to Gramsci, what most distinguished pre-revolutionary Russia from the West was the relative weakness of civil society in Russia and its relative strength in Europe and the United States. Neither the tsarist aristocracy, nor the short-lived government of the liberal bourgeoisie under Alexander Kerensky during 1917 just prior to the Bolshevik revolution, had been able to exercise the intellectual and moral leadership necessary to unite the masses of the Russian populace under its hegemony.

By contrast, in the more developed countries of the West, the equilibrium between state and civil society tended to be much stronger than in transitional or primarily agrarian countries like pre-revolutionary Russia. The development of capitalism in the West had been accompanied by the growth of an increasingly complex civil society—the development of a skilled labor force, the importance of knowledge and education in production, the role of the mass media, and the availability of more sophisticated techniques for the manipulation of "public opinion" (Boggs 1976: 48). Gramsci cited the successful liberal regimes of the nineteenth century in England, France, and the United States as examples where the bourgeoisie had succeeded in establishing hegemony.

Unlike these countries, nineteenth-century Germany and post-Renaissance Italy were cited as examples where the hegemony of the ruling groups was incomplete due in large part to the fact that the bourgeois revolutions in these countries had not succeeded in translating themselves into genuinely "national–popular" movements.[5] In Italy especially, civil society lacked the cohesion that had developed in England and the United States. From at least the time of Machiavelli, when the stirrings of national unification had first appeared, Italy had experienced sharp social–political fragmentation with division among the city-states, between religious and anti-clerical interests, between the urban North and the rural South, between industrial capitalism and feudal agrarianism (Boggs 1976: 49).

Roman Catholicism, the one form of ideology that was national in scope, had actually served to thwart efforts at national unification. Catholicism was ultimately cosmopolitan rather than nationalistic in its ideological orientation. Politically it was aligned with the Papal States and played a sectarian role in resisting the movement for national unification under the leadership of the liberal bourgeoisie of the North. Aside from the omnipresent influence of Catholicism, which did not serve as a basis for the organization of a national–popular collective will, there was no shared system of values that provided widespread legitimacy to dominant institutions and interests (Boggs 1976: 49; Gramsci 1971: 53–120). Even the *Risorgimento* or "resurgence" of nationalist sentiment, which succeeded in achieving a formal unification of Italy in the mid-nineteenth century, failed to establish an ideological bond between elites and popular groups that would make possible an extensive national community. It lacked the "Jacobin" force necessary to unite the various social groupings in Italy under its hegemony (Boggs 1976: 49–50).[6]

Thus, while the ruling groups in Western societies had not been equally successful in establishing their hegemony, it remained the case that civil society was far more developed in the West, even in Germany and Italy, than it had been in Russia at the time of the 1917 revolution. And it was precisely the weakness of civil society in Russia that helped to account for the success of the Bolsheviks. The state had rested upon such a fragile foundation that it was relatively easily toppled by a small organized revolutionary group.

> In Russia the State was everything, civil society was primordial and gelatinous; in the West, there was a proper relation between state and civil society, and when the state trembled a sturdy structure of civil society was at once revealed. The state was only an outer ditch, behind which there stood a powerful system of fortresses and earthworks: more or less numerous from one state to the next, it goes without saying—but this precisely necessitated an accurate reconnaissance of each individual country.
>
> (Gramsci 1971: 238)

In this passage Gramsci is using the term "state" in its conventional sense to mean government. But it is important to realize that in the context of his thought as a whole, Gramsci does not see the state and civil society as entirely separate but rather as complementary and mutually reinforcing spheres through which a dominant group exercises its hegemony. He often uses the term "integral state" to designate this relationship between "political" and "civil" society. As Peter Thomas explains,

> Civil society is the terrain upon which social classes compete for social and political leadership or hegemony over other social classes. Such hegemony is guaranteed, however, "in the last instance", by capture of the legal monopoly of violence embodied in the institutions of political society. Understood in this integral sense, Gramsci argued in March 1933, "the State is the entire complex of practical and theoretical activities with which the ruling class not only justifies and maintains its dominance, but manages to win the active consent of those over whom it rules".
> (Thomas 2010: 137–138; see Gramsci 1971: 244)

Thomas also cites a famous passage from the *Prison Notebooks* in which Gramsci writes that:

> the general notion of the State includes elements which need to be referred back to the notion of civil society (in the sense that one might say that the State = political society + civil society, in other words hegemony armoured with coercion).
> (Thomas 2010: 138; Gramsci 1971: 263)[7]

The lesson for political strategy to be drawn from all of this was that revolutionary politics in the West would have to consist not only in a struggle for the control of the government, but also largely in ideological struggle. In terms of the military metaphor used by Gramsci, the nature of political power in advanced capitalist countries prevents its overthrow by a "war of movement" or "frontal attack" on the state apparatus. Rather, a socialist transformation of society will be the result of a long "war of position" involving the gradual occupation of positions of intellectual and moral leadership within the institutions of civil society (1971: 238–239). Civil society would be the terrain on which classes contest for ideological and political power; a socialist revolution would be a process rather than an event (Boggs 1976: 53; Thomas 2010: 171–173).

Thus while orthodox Marxists had conceived the nature of the revolutionary transition primarily in terms of an economic transformation resulting from inevitable historical processes, and while Lenin understood revolution primarily in terms of a political transformation brought about by a seizure of governmental power, Gramsci came to view the revolutionary process primarily in terms of intellectual and moral transformation brought about by ideological struggle in the sphere of civil society. Before armed struggle for control of governmental power became meaningful and effective, the position of the ruling class would have to be demystified at the level of popular beliefs. A new worldview and ethic would have to be created and diffused throughout society. Indeed, Gramsci arrived at the remarkable conclusion that "The foundation of a directive class [*class dirigente*] (i.e. of a State) is equivalent to the creation of a *Weltanschauung*" (1971: 381). Conflicts over ideas and values could no longer be dismissed by Marxists but would have to be recognized as political forces that shape the nature of the struggle for power between competing social groups (Boggs 1976: 40–41). It is to a consideration of what Gramsci ultimately came to regard as the *religious* nature of the struggle for hegemony that we now turn.

Philosophy, Religion, and Common Sense in the Struggle for Intellectual and Moral Reformation

One of the most striking features of Gramsci's thought was his view that Marxism is not only a philosophy, political program, or conception of history, but also a new secular religion that seeks to integrate its worldview and practical ethic into a distinctive culture. Gramsci stated his conception of the "philosophy of praxis" as a modern intellectual and moral reformation in the notes for his projected work on the nature and tasks of the Communist Party, a work for which he planned the Machiavellian title *The Modern Prince*.

> An important part of *The Modern Prince* will have to be devoted to the question of intellectual and moral reform, that is, to the question of religion or world-view … The modern Prince [the Communist Party] must be and cannot but be the proclaimer and organiser of an intellectual and moral reform, which also means creating the terrain for a subsequent development of the national-popular collective will towards the realisation of a superior, total form of modern civilisation.
>
> (Gramsci 1971: 132–133)

Gramsci's interpretation of Marxism as a secular religion owes more to the influence of Georges Sorel (1847–1922) and Benedetto Croce (1866–1952) than it does to Marx and Engels. Indeed, it was from Sorel that Gramsci borrowed the "conception of the philosophy of praxis as a modern popular reformation" (1971: 395).

> Sorel has taken from Renan the concept of the necessity of an intellectual and moral reformation; he has affirmed … that great historical movements are often represented by a modern culture, etc. It seems to me, though, that a conception of this kind is implicit in Sorel when he uses primitive Christianity as a touchstone, in a rather literary way it is

true, but nevertheless with more than a grain of truth; with mechanical and often contrived references, but nevertheless with occasional flashes of profound intuition.

(Gramsci 1971: 395)[8]

The idea of intellectual and moral reformation is important for Gramsci, because it designates a transformation of the way in which the mass of the population conceptualizes the role of the individual, his or her place in society and relationship to other human beings, to God, to the economy, and to politics. It is a change in the conception of the world held by most people comparable to that brought about by primitive Christianity, the Protestant Reformation, or the French Revolution (Sassoon 1982a: 14). According to Gramsci, it is just this sort of wholesale transformation of worldview and ethos—"conceptions of the world and norms of conduct"— that the philosophy of praxis seeks to bring about (Wainwright 2010).

To achieve such a transformation of consciousness and society, it would be necessary for the revolutionary party to accomplish two tasks. In the first place, it would have to combat the *philosophy of the philosophers* in order to rally the intellectuals of subordinate classes away from the masters of traditional thought. At the same time, it would also have to combat *common sense, popular religion*, and *folklore* in an effort to diffuse a superior culture among the masses (Portelli 1974: 286; Crehan 2002: 98–119).

The philosophy of praxis had two tasks to perform: to combat modern ideologies in their most refined form, in order to be able to constitute its own group of intellectuals; and to educate the popular masses, whose culture was medieval.

(Gramsci 1971: 392)

It was in connection with the first of these tasks that Gramsci carried out his critique of Benedetto Croce.

The Philosophy of the Philosophers

Benedetto Croce was the dominant influence in Italian intellectual life during Gramsci's lifetime and for many years thereafter. Indeed, Croce's preeminent position in the cultural and political life of Italy and throughout much of Europe led Gramsci to describe him as the "lay pope" of secular intellectual life (Gramsci 1973: 204). While the Church remained socialism's biggest competitor for the loyalty of the masses, Gramsci viewed Croce's brand of philosophical idealism and political liberalism as the most dangerous adversary in the struggle for the loyalty of the intellectuals.

Robert Bellah has provided a valuable key for understanding the complicated relationship between Croce and Gramsci by suggesting that each of them may be viewed as a kind of prophet of modernity. Both were seeking to address the spiritual and moral crisis brought about by secularization and the decline of traditional religion and morality.

> Both Croce and Gramsci, viewed in the proper light, can be seen as lawgivers and even as prophets. Both were intensely concerned with the ethical and political orders of Italian society. Both had a vision of a good normative order they hoped to persuade their society to adopt. Both based their norm giving or lawgiving on a fundamental conception of reality to which they gave ultimate respect and that they invoked as legitimation for their normative demands; so they can rightly be called prophets. To Croce the historical realization of liberty was the highest good; to Gramsci it was the dialectic of socialist liberation.
>
> (Bellah 1980: 87)

Croce's critique of positivism and his stress on the importance of intuition and imagination in understanding the processes of historical change and of artistic creation made him a leading figure in what H.S. Hughes (1977) has described as "the reorientation of European social thought" that was taking place between 1890 and 1930. In the 1890s Croce had immersed himself in the study of Marx and, for a brief period, he had even regarded himself as a Marxist. Ultimately, however, he abandoned Marxism as a result of his disenchantment with orthodox Marxism's economic determinism as well as because of his lack of sympathy with the revolutionary politics of the workers' movement. Nonetheless, it was through his study of Marx that Croce had been led back to an interest in the philosophy of Hegel, and it was as a representative of neo-Hegelian historicism that Croce was to become best known (see Hughes 1977: 200–229; Finocchiaro 1988).[9]

Where Croce had more in common with Hegel than with Marx was in the view that history was the history of the human spirit and that the key to historical understanding was in the development of the human soul rather than in the development of the material conditions of life. He shared with Hegel the belief that history was the history of freedom and that each successive stage of historical development was marked by a further realization of a person's potential for liberty (Joll 1977: 33).

In 1914 Croce had written a letter to Georges Sorel in which he claimed that the great social problem of the modern age was to learn to "live without religions," that is, without traditional "confessional" religion. Later, in his *History of Europe in the Nineteenth Century* (1932), Croce claimed that traditional religion, along with the various nineteenth-century ideologies that had sought to replace it, had been undermined by the crassly materialistic environment of post-1870 "Bismarckian" Europe (Adamson: 1987/8: 326). This gave rise to a crisis of meaning and authority that no religion or ideology had yet succeeded in resolving.

In the face of this crisis, Croce dedicated himself to the revival of the liberal tradition. He believed that liberalism could be refashioned to serve as a secular "religion of liberty," and the entirety of Croce's philosophical and historical work was calculated to advance this aim (Adamson 1987/8: 326). Croce contrasted his own brand of "liberalism" with "democracy," which was associated with the eighteenth century and the French Revolution, aspects of which Gramsci would describe favorably as "Jacobinism" (Bellah, 1980: 98). Croce regarded both "democracy" and "liberalism" as "lay" or secular "religions." But "democracy" was mechanical, intellectualistic, and abstractly egalitarian while the "liberalism" of the early nineteenth century with which he identified was personal, idealistic, and historically organic:

> The democrats in their political ideal postulated a religion of quantity, of mechanics, of calculating reason or of nature, like that of the eighteenth century; the liberals, a religion of quality, of activity, of spirituality, such as that which had risen in the beginning of the nineteenth century: so that even in this case, the conflict was one of religious faiths.
>
> (Croce cited in Bellah 1980: 98)

Thus, Croce's response to the spiritual and moral crisis brought about by secularization was to define liberalism itself as a secular religion capable of providing the sense of meaning and purpose that had been lost in the modern world. In keeping with this project, Croce opened his *History of Europe in the Nineteenth Century* with a chapter titled "The Religion of Liberty." After describing various features of liberalism as it came to be expressed in the early nineteenth century, he writes:

> Now he who gathers together and considers all these characteristics of the liberal ideal does not hesitate to call it what it was: a "religion." He calls it so, of course, because he looks for what is essential and intrinsic in every religion, which always lies in the concept of reality and an ethics that conforms to this concept ... Nothing more was needed to give them a religious character, since personifications, myths, legends, dogmas, rites, propitiations, expiations, priestly classes, pontifical robes, and the like do not belong to the intrinsic, and are taken out from particular religions and set up as requirements for every religion with ill effect.
>
> (Croce cited in Bellah 1980: 88; Croce 1953: 18)

In a subsequent chapter titled "Opposing Religious Faiths," Croce goes on to present Catholicism and socialism as the chief competitors to the religion of liberty (Bellah 1980: 88; Croce 1953: 20–41). Catholicism was an intellectually and politically outmoded worldview, suitable perhaps for the primitive needs and sensibilities of the peasants, but utterly incapable of accommodating itself to the scientific and political realities of the modern world. Marxism is viewed in a similar fashion. While Karl Marx had "created the new 'religion of the masses' in the same sense in which Paul of Tarsus created Christianity" (Croce cited in Bellah 1980: 102), Croce viewed Marxism as a vulgar and unsophisticated worldview and ethic on a par with popular Catholicism. Marxism played the same role among the industrial working class that popular Catholicism played among the peasantry. Neither was capable of providing an intellectually compelling worldview and ethic for modernity.

Gramsci found much in Croce's philosophy that he could enlist as an ally in his own struggle against orthodox Marxism. It was from Croce that Gramsci derived a conception of culture that was far deeper and more complex than that of many of his fellow socialists. He was also indebted to Croce for an awareness of the limitations of positivism and of the cruder forms of historical materialism propagated by many contemporary Marxists (Joll 1977: 34; Finocchiaro 1988). In contrast to the reigning forms of positivism, Croce's philosophy gave a sense of meaning and moral purpose to the study of history. Moreover, Croce's view of history embraced all human activity—art, economics, philosophy—so that to study history was to study the whole of life (Joll 1977: 33). What is more significant for the present discussion was Croce's influence on Gramsci's conception of religion and on his re-conceptualization of Marxism itself according to a religious paradigm (Finocchiaro 1988: 11–20).

Gramsci followed Croce in distinguishing between "religion in the confessional sense" and "religion" understood in the "lay" or secular sense. When Croce and Gramsci referred to "religion in the confessional sense," they had in mind the historical religions of the world as represented especially by Christianity. For Gramsci "traditional" or "confessional" religion is characterized by three constitutive elements: first, the belief in one or several personal divinities that transcend terrestrial and temporal conditions; second, the sense that humanity is dependent upon these superior beings for the government of life and the world; and third, the existence of a system of cultic relationships between humanity and the gods (Gramsci 1995: 9; Portelli 1973: 11). Insofar as traditional or confessional religions are characterized by supernaturalism and by the mythological or "non-scientific" manner in which they present reality, they are regarded as primitive and inferior forms of consciousness corresponding to the historical infancy of the human race (Portelli 1974: 24). Religion in the traditional or confessional sense is contrasted with the secular or "lay" definition of religion as "a conception of the world which has become a norm of life" (Gramsci 1971: 344). Both Croce and Gramsci were preoccupied with the creation of a new secular religion, a rational or "immanent" conception of the world, which could take the place of outmoded systems of beliefs and values.

Gramsci thus freely appropriated aspects of Croce's philosophy for his own thinking. As he wrote from prison, "Croce's thought must at least be appreciated as a valuable instrument, and so it can be said that he directed attention energetically to the facts of culture and thought in the development of history, to the function of the great intellectuals in the organic life of civil society and the State" (Gramsci cited in Joll 1977: 35).[10]

Yet despite Gramsci's appreciation of the breadth and grandeur—what he described as the "Goethean" aspect—of Croce's thought (Joll 1977: 34), he was nonetheless highly critical of Croce for both philosophical and political reasons. At the level of philosophy, Gramsci's critique of Croce's idealism reproduced Marx's critique of Hegel. Gramsci believed that Croce transposed concrete social conflicts into conflicts between concepts at the level of ideas. In so doing, Crocean idealism became an ideological apparatus justifying abstract and ahistorical values. Metaphysical and historical speculation became a substitute for political struggle. Gramsci sought to debunk Croce's ideological and political pretensions while incorporating elements of his system into his own effort to renovate Marxism (Salamini 1974: 365). At the level of politics, Gramsci was critical of Croce not only because of his increasingly anti-Marxist position, but because of the politically ambiguous and passive character of the liberalism entailed by Croce's highly speculative philosophical system.

Before the First World War, Croce's sympathy for the Italian left, his revaluation of the Italian romantic tradition from Vico to the present, and his opposition to contemporary positivism had led Gramsci to evaluate his political and cultural influence in a favorable light (editors in Gramsci 1971: xxiv). But over time Gramsci came to believe that Croce's influence had become increasingly reactionary. For example, Gramsci had admired Croce's initial opposition to the First World War, writing that when "so many intellectuals lost their heads ... Croce remained imperturbable in his serenity and in the affirmation of his faith that 'metaphysically evil could not prevail and that history is rationality'" (Gramsci cited in Joll 1977: 34). But too often this detachment and sense of being above the struggle led to a refusal to accept responsibility, to what Gramsci described as *ponzio-pilatismo*, the attitude of Pontius Pilate washing his hands of responsibility and disowning the consequences of his judgments and actions (Joll 1977: 34). Thus while Croce had initially argued against intervention during the period of Italy's neutrality, "when the government's decision had gone against him, he duly turned up in the Senate to vote for war, and during the conflict itself he maintained an attitude that was 'correct' if something short of enthusiastic" (Hughes 1977: 214). Ultimately, Gramsci concluded that

> Croce's attitude during the war can be compared only to that of the Pope, who was the head of the bishops who blessed the German and Austrian arms, as he was of those who blessed the arms of the Italians and French, without there being any contradiction in it.
>
> (Gramsci cited in Hughes 1977: 214)

From Gramsci's point of view, Croce's role became increasingly pernicious during the Fascist era. Croce had initially given Mussolini's regime his qualified endorsement as a revitalizing force in the national life. But by 1925 he had begun to distance himself from the regime and to withdraw from political activity. Unlike his fellow philosopher Giovanni Gentile (1875–1944), Croce never played a direct or active part in the elaboration of Fascist cultural policy. Yet even so,

> the fact remains that he did support the regime at the outset and that the theoretical character of his later opposition was of a singularly insipid and depoliticising kind, whose effect on the intellectual strata subject to Crocean influence was at best to inspire a certain withdrawal from Fascist vulgarity, but which more often promoted a habit of "justificationism" with regard to the regime far more extensive than any provided by Hegel's supposed glorification of the Prussian monarchy.
>
> (editors in Gramsci 1971: xxiv)

James Joll lends support to this harsh judgment when he writes that in Croce's writings during the Fascist period one finds "a combination of liberalism and faith in an undefined world-spirit" that "often led to a rather empty high-minded belief that somehow everything would turn out all right" (Joll 1977: 33).[11]

Thus, for all his indebtedness to Croce, Gramsci rejected what he saw as the politically conservative and elitist implications of Croce's thought. Croce's philosophy remained speculative—a self-styled philosophy of spirit. Marxism, by contrast, was the philosophy of praxis, a philosophy that found its justification in practical activity (Joll 1977: 34). For Croce, the historical validity of a *Weltanschauung* was determined solely by the degree of rationality it exhibited and by the authority of its expositors, while for Gramsci what was important was a worldview's intrinsic capacity to mobilize, politicize, and reform the thinking and activity of the largest number of individuals (Salamini 1974: 69). In contrast to Croce, Gramsci insisted that an intellectual revolution could not be carried out simply by confronting one philosophy with another. Not only ideas, but the social forces behind them would have to be confronted (editors in Gramsci 1971: 321).

Nonetheless, Gramsci largely agreed with the manner in which Croce defined the intellectual and moral crisis of the modern secular age. In one of his letters from prison, he recognized that both Croce's liberalism and his own effort to reformulate Marxism were attempts to deal with the same fundamental problems of historical change and human development.

> We are all to some degree part of the movement of moral and intellectual reform which in Italy stemmed from Benedetto Croce, and whose first premise was that modern man can and should live without the help of religion—I mean of course without revealed religion, positivist religion, mythological religion, or whatever brand one cares to name.
>
> (Gramsci cited in Joll 1977: 35)

Like Croce, Gramsci saw traditional religion being left behind as humankind matured toward autonomy and toward a "modern conception of the world"

(Fulton 1987: 201–202). Already in his early writings he had made a sympathetic note of Croce's contention that secular philosophy could in principle supply the same consolations as had confessional religion (Adamson 1987/8: 326). He also shared Croce's view that all commitments possess an element of belief or faith, an active conviction and commitment (Fulton 1987: 201–202).

In a passage strikingly reminiscent of Emile Durkheim's observation that "the old gods are growing old or are already dead, and others are not yet born" (1965: 475 cited in Adamson 1987/8: 338), Gramsci sums up the crisis of meaning in a secular age.

> That aspect of the modern crisis which is bemoaned as a "wave of materialism" is related to what is called the "crisis of authority" … the great masses have become detached from their traditional ideologies, and no longer believe what they used to believe, etc. The crisis consists precisely in the fact that the old is dying and the new cannot be born; in this interregnum a wide variety of morbid symptoms appear.
>
> (Gramsci cited in Adamson 1987/8: 327;
> see Gramsci 1971: 275–276)[12]

Gramsci thus joined Croce in posing the crisis of modernity in religious and ethical terms and in emphasizing the need for a "coherent, unitary, nationally diffused 'conception of life and man,' a 'lay religion,' a philosophy that has become precisely a 'culture,' that is, generated an ethic, a way of life, a civil and individual form of conduct" (Gramsci cited in Adamson 1987/8: 327). But of course Gramsci denied that Croce's brand of liberalism was capable of providing such a worldview and ethic. On the contrary, Croce's philosophy was little more than an "atheism for aristocrats" (Gramsci cited in Adamson 1987/8: 328). Croce believed that only an elite of superior intellects is capable of a rational conception of the world while the masses will continue to need "traditional" religion. In this connection Gramsci wrote of Croce's "Malthusian attitude" toward religion, his fear of, and contempt for, the masses (Gramsci 1971: 132).

Gramsci also compared Crocean idealism to the elitism and cosmopolitanism that had been characteristic of the Italian Renaissance. Unlike the Protestant Reformation, which Gramsci interpreted as a mass popular movement, the Renaissance had remained limited in its impact precisely because it was cut off from the people. Marxism, on the other hand, resembled the Protestant Reformation, an intellectual and social movement that ultimately had a more far-reaching and thorough-going impact on world history than had the Renaissance. Unlike Croce's philosophy, "the philosophy of praxis, with its vast mass movement, has represented and does represent an historical process similar to the Reformation, in contrast to liberalism, which reproduces a Renaissance which is narrowly limited to restricted intellectual groups …" (Gramsci 1971: 132).

Croce is, in essence, anti-confessional (we cannot say anti-religious given his definition of what constitutes religion) and for a large number of Italian and European intellectuals his philosophy ... has constituted a real and proper intellectual and moral reform of a "Renaissance'" type ... But Croce has not "gone to the people", has not wanted to become a "national" element (just as the Renaissance men were not, unlike the Lutherans and Calvinists), has not wanted to create a group of disciples who ... could popularise his philosophy in his place and try to make it into an educational element right from the primary school stage (and thus educational for the simple worker and peasant, that is to say for the simple man in the street). Perhaps this was not possible, but it was worth the trouble of trying to do it, and not having tried is also significant.

(Gramsci 1995: 408; see also Gramsci 1971: 132 note 14)

Croce's philosophy is an example of what Gramsci described as an "arbitrary ideology." An arbitrary ideology is "rationalistic, or 'willed'" and refers to "the arbitrary elucubrations of particular individuals" (Gramsci 1971: 376–377). Gramsci has in mind here the philosophies of individual philosophers like Croce, Giovanni Gentile, Gabriele D'Annunzio (1863–1938) and their followers who articulate "conceptions of the world" that are not organic to a fundamental social group and which fail to be taken up by a mass historical movement but remain the property of relatively small coteries of intellectuals.

modern culture, especially that marked by idealism, does not manage to elaborate a popular culture or to give a moral and scientific content to its own school programmes, which remain abstract and theoretical schemas. It remains the culture of a restricted intellectual aristocracy ...

(Gramsci 1971: 393)[13]

By contrast, the philosophy of praxis is, or aspires to be, an "organic ideology," an ideology "in the highest sense." Gramsci writes that "in its highest sense," ideology refers to "a conception of the world that is implicitly manifest in art, in law, in economic activity and in all manifestations of individual and collective life" (1971: 328). An organic ideology is "the necessary superstructure of a particular structure" (1971: 376). It is "a conception of the world," a "philosophy" that has become "a cultural movement, a 'religion', and 'faith'" that has "produced a form of practical activity or will in which the philosophy is contained as an implicit theoretical 'premiss'" (1971: 328).

To the extent that ideologies are historically necessary they have a validity which is "psychological"; they "organise" human masses, and create terrain on which men move, acquire consciousness of their position, struggle, etc. To the extent that they are arbitrary they only create individual "movements", polemics and so on ...

(1971: 377)

The fundamental question facing "any cultural movement which aimed to replace common sense and old conceptions of the world in general" was the question of how new worldviews and ethics are diffused throughout a society.

> What are the influential factors in the process of diffusion (which is also one of a substitution of the old conception, and, very often, of combining old and new), how do they act, and to what extent? Is it the rational form in which the new conception is expounded and presented? Or is it the authority ... of the expositor and the thinkers and experts whom the expositor calls in in his support? Or the fact of belonging to the same organisation as the man who upholds the new conception ...?
>
> (Gramsci 1971: 338)

Gramsci rejected the idea that a transformation of popular consciousness could be accomplished simply by means of rational argumentation. For if commitment to a worldview and ethic was simply a matter of rational debate, an individual would be forced to change his beliefs any time he encountered someone who was better educated and who subscribed to a contrary point of view (Gramsci 1971: 339).

> Imagine the intellectual position of the man of the people: he has formed his own opinions, convictions, criteria of discrimination, standards of conduct. Anyone with a superior intellectual formation with a point of view opposed to his can put forward arguments better than he and really tear him to pieces logically and so on. But should the man of the people change his opinions just because of this? Just because he cannot impose himself in a bout of argument? In that case he might find himself having to change every day, or every time he meets an ideological adversary who is his intellectual superior. On what elements, therefore, can his philosophy be founded? And in particular his philosophy in the form which has the greatest importance for his standards of conduct?
>
> (Gramsci 1971: 339)

Gramsci was convinced that no worldview and ethic, Marxism included, could ever gain ascendency simply because of the logical consistency of its analysis or the "knowledge" it could supply, nor because of the theoretical contributions of great thinkers, as important as these might be (Boggs 1976: 66–67). On the contrary,

> The most important element is undoubtedly one whose character is determined not by reason but by *faith*. But faith in whom, or in what? In particular in the social group to which he belongs, in so far as in a diffuse way it thinks as he does. The man of the people thinks that so many like-thinking people can't be wrong, not so radically, as the man he is arguing with would like him to believe; he thinks that, while he himself,

admittedly, is not able to uphold and develop his arguments as well as the opponent, in his group there is someone who could do this and who could certainly argue better than the particular man he has against him; and he remembers, indeed, hearing expounded, discursively, coherently, in a way that left him convinced, the reasons behind his faith. He has no concrete memory of the reasons and could not repeat them, but he knows that reasons exist, because he has heard them expounded, and was convinced by them. The fact of having once suddenly seen the light and been convinced is the permanent reason for his reasons persisting, even if the arguments in its favour cannot be readily produced.

(Gramsci 1971: 339, emphasis added)

Thus, the diffusion of new conceptions of the world ultimately "takes place for political (that is, in the last analysis, social) reasons" (Gramsci 1971: 339).

In acquiring one's conception of the world one always belongs to a particular grouping which is that of all the social elements which share the same mode of thinking and acting. We are all conformists of some conformism or other, always man-in-the-mass or collective man. The question is this: of what historical type is the conformism, the mass humanity to which one belongs? When one's conception of the world is not critical and coherent but disjointed and episodic, one belongs simultaneously to a multiplicity of mass human groups. The personality is strangely composite: it contains Stone Age elements and principles of a more advanced science, prejudices from all past phases of history at the local level and intuitions of a future philosophy which will be that of a human race united the world over.

(Gramsci 1971: 342)

Gramsci believed that people were basically conformists who tended to adopt the norms, ideology, and mode of behavior of their fellows in an uncritical fashion. The worldviews and morals of the people were for the most part incoherent and unreflective, and it was the task of the revolutionary political party to enable them to develop a coherent, self-conscious, and critical ideology for the first time (Kertzer 1979: 325–326).

To criticise one's own conception of the world means therefore to make it a coherent unity and to raise it to the level reached by the most advanced thought in the world. It therefore also means criticism of all previous philosophy, in so far as this has left stratified deposits in popular philosophy. The starting-point of critical elaboration is the consciousness of what one really is, and is "knowing thyself" as a product of the historical process to date which has deposited in you an infinity of traces, without leaving an inventory.

(Gramsci 1971: 324)

Thus, for Gramsci, revolutionary politics, the task of transforming society, was not a mere technical question of seizing power. Rather it was a matter of determining the means by which to awaken faith in the socialist project and mobilize the will of the nation or people. The task of ethical–political science was not simply the disinterested search for knowledge about the logic of political behavior, but rather the arousal of popular passions and the activation of a national–popular collective will.

It is here that we come to the second task mentioned above, that of "educating the masses whose culture is medieval." For in order to realize a true ideological bloc of the subordinate groups in society, the philosophy of praxis would not only have to confront the philosophy of the philosophers—it would also have to confront the "spontaneous philosophy" of the masses, which is expressed in common sense, popular religion, and folklore (Gramsci 1971: 323). The critique of "common sense" and that of the "philosophy of the philosophers" are therefore viewed as complementary aspects of a single ideological struggle (editors in Gramsci 1971: 322).

Common Sense, Popular Religion, Folklore

Gramsci was highly critical of those Marxist writers who seemed to assume that "the elaboration of an original philosophy of the popular masses is to be opposed to the great systems of traditional philosophy and the religion of the leaders of the clergy—i.e. the conception of the world of the intellectuals and of high culture" (Gramsci 1971: 419).[14]

> In reality these systems are unknown to the multitude and have no direct influence on its way of thinking and acting. This does not mean of course that they are altogether without influence, but it is influence of a different kind. These systems influence the popular masses as an external political force, an element of cohesive force exercised by the ruling classes and therefore an element of subordination to an external hegemony. This limits the original thought of the popular masses in a negative direction, without having the positive effect of a vital ferment of interior transformation of what the masses think in an embryonic and chaotic form about the world and life.
>
> (Gramsci 1971: 419–420)

Besides offering an alternative to the great systems of the philosophers and theologians, the philosophy of praxis would eventually have to face the more important and ultimately more difficult task of opposing a coherent superior conception of the world to the primitive, disparate, and contradictory common sense of the masses (Portelli 1974: 274). For Gramsci, the creation of a new "common sense" signifies the creation of a "new culture and a new philosophy which takes root in popular consciousness with the same force and the same imperative character as the traditional beliefs" that constitute common sense (Gramsci cited in Portelli 1974: 287).

Gramsci used the term "common sense" in order to designate the uncritical and largely unconscious way of perceiving and understanding the world that has become common in any given epoch (editors in Gramsci 1971: 322). He describes common sense as the "philosophy of non-philosophers" and as the "'folklore' of philosophy" (1971: 419). Common sense is "the conception of the world which is uncritically absorbed by the various social and cultural environments in which the moral individuality of the average man is developed" (1971: 419).

Correspondingly, Gramsci uses the phrase "good sense" to refer to the practical, but not necessarily rational or scientific, attitude that in English is usually called common sense. Broadly speaking, "common sense" means the incoherent set of generally held assumptions and beliefs common to any given society, while "good sense" means practical empirical common sense in the English usage of the term (editors in Gramsci 1971: 322–323).[15]

Common sense is not a single univocal conception; rather, "it takes countless different forms" (Gramsci 1971: 419).

> Every social stratum has its own "common sense" and its own "good sense", which are basically the most widespread conception of life and man. Every philosophical current leaves behind a sedimentation of "common sense": this is the document of its historical effectiveness. Common sense is not something rigid and immobile, but is continually transforming itself, enriching itself with scientific ideas and with philosophical opinions which have entered ordinary life. "Common sense" is the folklore of philosophy, and is always halfway between folklore properly speaking and the philosophy, science, and economics of the specialists. Common sense creates the folklore of the future, that is as a relatively rigid phase of popular knowledge at a given place and time.
>
> (Gramsci 1971: 326 note 5)

Thus, common sense conforms to the social and cultural position of "those masses whose philosophy it is" (1971: 419). Among its fundamental characteristics is that it consists of fragmentary, incoherent, and sometimes contradictory assumptions and beliefs, even within the mind of a single individual (1971: 419).

Nevertheless, common sense must not be thought of as "false consciousness" nor as ideology in a merely negative sense. It contains elements of truth as well as elements of misrepresentation. Common sense is a complex ideological sedimentation, some aspects of which can and must be incorporated in the process of cultural revolution: "What was said above does not mean that there are no truths in common sense. It means rather that common sense is an ambiguous, contradictory and multiform concept, and that to refer to common sense as a confirmation of truth is a nonsense" (Gramsci 1971: 423; Portelli 1974: 286).

The ethical–political significance of common sense is twofold. On the one hand, many of its elements contribute to people's subordination by making situations of inequality and oppression appear to them as natural and unchangeable. On the other hand, Gramsci believed it was crucial that Marxism should not present itself as an abstract philosophy but rather should seek to enter people's common sense, giving them a more critical understanding of their own situation (Forgacs 1988: 421).

The historical task of theory was to politicize the incoherent and fragmentary ideas of "common sense," which takes on multiple characteristics in bourgeois society, instead of searching for a pure revolutionary truth that looks like a "baroque form of Platonic idealism."

> Indeed, because by its nature it tends towards being a mass philosophy, the philosophy of praxis can only be conceived in a polemical form and in the form of perpetual struggle. Nonetheless the starting point must always be that common sense which is the spontaneous philosophy of the multitude and which has to be made ideologically coherent.
>
> (Gramsci 1971: 421 cited in Boggs 1976: 65)

In addition to common sense, "religion" is another form in which the "spontaneous philosophy" of the masses is expressed. Traditional or "confessional" religion "is an element of fragmented common sense," whereas the philosophy of the philosophers is "intellectual order which neither religion nor common sense can be" (1971: 325). Yet religion is not reducible to common sense, because it is a form of total social praxis (Fulton 1987: 206).

As we will see in more detail below, Gramsci distinguished between the "religion of the people" or "popular religion" and the "religion of the intellectuals" (Fulton 1987: 203–207; Crehan 2002: 107–119). By "popular religion" Gramsci refers to the beliefs, morals, and practices that express in a "religious" way (that is, a pre-scientific, otherworldly, supernaturalistic way) the needs of workers, peasants, the middle classes, and various other social groups. It gives a religious interpretation to the immediate experience of nature and human relationships (Fulton 1987: 201). The "religion of the intellectuals," on the other hand, refers to the theology and dogma of the world religions in their elaborated and unified form. It is the religion of priests and theologians, religion in its organizational mode with its clerical and lay functionaries (Fulton 1987: 205). Such an elaborated and unified intellectual system is also and inevitably a source of political power.

> [A religion] could not have become elaborated intellectually, morally, and organizationally unless it had been in the past, or has become in the present, a hegemonic form in society, a means of social control at the level of the mind and the heart. There is a direct connection in Gramsci

between social control and intellectual elaboration. That which is hegemonic in the thought and behavior of people is also an intellectually detailed and integrated system of interpretation and organization, though this integration and detail exist *outside* the people and *in* the intellectuals.

(Fulton 1987: 205)

The religion of the people draws upon the religion of the intellectuals, but it does not simply reproduce the religion of the intellectuals at a lower level of sophistication. Rather it draws upon a wide range of other sources from the common cultural experience as well as from systematized and intellectual religion (Fulton 1987: 205). And indeed, as we will see in the next chapter, the religion of the people and the religion of the intellectuals have often been at odds with one another historically.

Gramsci's attitude toward religion was ambivalent. As Roland Boer remarks, "Gramsci's writings seem free of polemic" when compared to the hostile and intensely anti-religious rhetoric of many Marxists. "Apart from the occasional wry comment, and a few attacks, Gramsci offers a measured analysis, seeking to understand the intricate web of political, social, moral and theological questions of the Church's inescapable place in Italian society" (Boer 2009: 216–217). On the one hand, he viewed Catholicism as the most serious threat to socialism on the Italian scene. He recognized that the Catholic Church presented a far greater cultural and political challenge to the philosophy of praxis than did the philosophy of someone like Benedetto Croce. "The Pope as leader and guide of the majority of Italian peasants and women is great, indeed the greatest political force in the country after the government, given that his authority and influence operate through a centralized and well-articulated organization" (Gramsci cited in Adamson 1987/8: 328). Shortly before his arrest in 1926, Gramsci wrote in the theses of the Communist Party Congress that the power the Church exercised over the peasant masses had to be destroyed as a precondition for the victorious struggle against capitalism. Many of Gramsci's writings, particularly though not exclusively his early newspaper articles, are clear in their anti-religious tone. He speaks of the "imbecile illusion of immortality" and looks forward to the success of "democratic Catholicism," which will result in the "suicide" of Catholicism and the "execution of God." With some exceptions, Gramsci's detestation of "Popes and Jesuits" continued unabated throughout his life (Gramsci cited in Fulton 1987: 201).

Yet at the same time, Gramsci appreciated the "necessary" role played by folk Catholicism in "rationalising the world and real life" and in providing "the general framework for real practical activity" (Gramsci 1971: 337; Kertzer 1979: 327). Gramsci developed this idea by noting the way in which the First World War had fomented new religious movements and a return to witchcraft.

The religious indifference of normal times, the absence of cultic practice, is not independence or liberation from idolatry. Religion is a need of the spirit. People feel so lost in the vastness of the world, so thrown about by forces they do not understand; and the complex of historical forces, artful and subtle as they are, so escapes the common sense that in the moments that matter only the person who has substituted religion with some other moral force succeeds in saving the self from disaster.

(Gramsci cited in Fulton 1987: 202)

Gramsci thus recognized the complexity of the Catholicism of the masses and did not see all religion in negative terms. As we have seen, Gramsci shared with both Sorel and Croce the view that all commitments possess an element of faith and an active belief and conviction. This is a feature that both religion and genuine socialism share. He also admired the Roman Catholic Church's historical organization and its long-enduring hegemony in European society. As we will see, he even believed that aspects of this experience could serve as models for Marxist praxis (Fulton 1987: 201–202). In this connection he contrasted primitive Christianity and the simple Christianity of the people with the "Jesuitized Christianity which had become a pure narcotic for the masses" (Gramsci cited in Kertzer 1979: 327).

Finally, in addition to common sense, and closely linked to popular religion, "folklore" is a third form in which the "spontaneous philosophy" of the masses is expressed. It is the least integrated, elaborated, and intellectually sophisticated form of popular consciousness. Gramsci most often used the term "folklore" to embrace the popular culture of subordinate groups in society and their interpretations of everyday experience at their own intellectual, moral, and religious level. Folklore consists of un-integrated bits and pieces from past popular religions and local cultures which live on in the customs, superstitions, entertainments, myths, and rituals of the common people. Folklore thus originates from sources other than the elaborated and systematic culture of the intellectuals or the philosophy, religion, and morality of the dominant groups in society (Fulton 1987: 206).

Again, as in the case of both common sense and popular religion, the ethical–political significance of folklore is ambiguous. On the one hand, folklore is fragmentary and contradictory. It consists of those residues of past cultures such as magic, witchcraft, and superstitions of all sorts, which must be combated and are best left dead and buried if the masses are to attain a rational conception of the world. At the same time, however, folklore is a source of popular resistance to the incursions of the philosophy and religion of the dominant social groups. In this connection, Gramsci recognized the peculiar irony of the fact that it was precisely the representatives of intellectual culture who record for posterity the contents of such folklore (Fulton 1987: 206).[16]

This complex account of ideology and social consciousness in terms of philosophy, the religion of the intellectuals, common sense, popular religion, and folklore provides the framework for Gramsci's more detailed inquiries into the ethical–political history of Christianity and for his reflections on the intellectual and moral tasks confronting political parties and movements for social change in the modern world. It is to a consideration of these inquiries and reflections that we now turn.

Notes

1 Kautsky was a leader of the German Social Democratic Party and a recognized spokesman for orthodoxy after Engels' death in 1895. Plekhanov was considered the "father of Russian Marxism" and was the first to characterize Marx's mature thought as "dialectical materialism." Kautsky's and Plekhanov's "orthodoxy" was apparent in their opposition to both Eduard Bernstein's "revisionist" Marxism and to Leninism. See Kolakowski (2005: 379–402; 620–639) and McLellan (2007: 21–43; 71–79) for a more extensive discussion of these two figures.

2 For discussion of the influence of positivism and evolutionism in Marxism see Hughes (1977) and McLellan (2007; 1987).

3 On the contrast between Gramsci's and Lenin's views of revolution, see Kolakowski (2005: 986–988).

4 For a concise account of the origins and development of the concept of hegemony in Gramsci's thought see Boothman (2011). For discussion of how Gramsci's concept of civil society differs from those of Hegel and Marx see Adamson (1987/8), Bobbio (1979), and Thomas (2010).

5 See Gramsci 1971: 82ff. for a discussion of the German case.

6 See below for more on Gramsci's use of the concepts of "national–popular" and "Jacobinism."

7 Discussion of the relationship between coercion, consent, the state, and civil society in Gramsci's thought is extensive. Among the most helpful, in addition to Thomas (2010), are Adamson (1987/8), Buttigieg (2005 and 2009), Crehan (2002: 99–105), and McLellan (2007: 203–210). We will return to this issue in chapter four.

8 As Gramsci indicates in this passage, Sorel himself adopted the concept of intellectual and moral reformation from Ernest Renan, whose *La Reforme Intellectuelle et Morale* was published in Paris in 1929. And elsewhere Gramsci explains that the notion ultimately came to Sorel via Renan from Pierre-Joseph Proudhon, whose *La Justice dans la Revolution et dans L'Eglise* was devoted to the search for a cultural, socialist, and anti-clerical transformation of popular consciousness. See Gramsci (1995: 25–26); Fulton (1987).

9 Joll (1977: 32) has shown that behind both Hegel's and Marx's conception of history as an all-embracing process with its own laws of development, Croce saw the figure of a fellow Neapolitan, the great eighteenth-century Italian thinker Giambattista Vico. Vico's thought had anticipated nineteenth-century historicism by viewing history as the cyclical working out of immutable laws and by maintaining that the study of history embraced the study of all aspects of human thought and human society. By the end of the nineteenth century, Vico had come to be recognized as an important forerunner of all historicist ways of thinking. Croce edited Vico's major work, *La Scienza Nuova*, and both Croce and Gramsci were much influenced by his ideas and his language.

10 As Joll goes on to note, the respect shown for Croce by Gramsci was not mutual. "When the first volumes of Gramsci's *Prison Notebooks* were published in the 1940s, Croce, then in his eighties and still a dominant figure on the Italian scene, dismissed them as 'roughly sketched and tentative ideas, self-questionings, conjectures and doubts often unfounded ... [lacking] that power of synthetic thought which discriminates, builds and integrates into a whole.' Yet, for all that, Croce's claim—characteristically having it both ways—that '*Gramsci era uno dei nostri*'—('Gramsci was one of us') remains true" (Joll 1977: 35–36).

11 For a more favourable evaluation of Croce's position vis-à-vis Fascism, see H.S. Hughes (1977: 215–229) who claims that by 1925 Croce had entered into "uncompromising opposition" to Mussolini's regime.

12 Parallels between Gramsci and Durkheim have been mentioned in passing by several writers, including Adamson (1987/8: 331) and Kertzer (1979). Mansueto (1988) discusses these parallels at some length. According to Adamson (1987/8: 338) there is no evidence that Gramsci knew of Durkheim or his work. However, Buttigieg (2011: 582) notes that, while in prison, Gramsci had a copy of Croce's *Historical Materialism and the Economics of Karl Marx*, which makes reference to "the Frenchman Durkheim" among other contemporary sociologists. I will return to a brief discussion of Gramsci and Durkheim on the question of the relationship between religion, ethics, and social order in chapter four.

13 Croce was minister of education in Giolitti's 1920/21 government, and introduced a draft bill to reorganize the national educational system; the bill provided for the reintroduction of religious instruction in the primary schools—something which had not existed since the 1859 Casati Act laid the basis for the educational system of post-Risorgimento Italy. In fact Giolitti withdrew the bill, but the main lines of it were taken up by Gentile when, as minister of education in the first Fascist government of 1922, he drew up the Gentile Act, which was passed in 1923 (editors in Gramsci 1971: 132). For more on Croce's and Gentile's school reform proposals see also editors in Gramsci (1971: 132, 393) and Gramsci (1995: 409). For thorough discussions of Gramsci's views on education, see Entwistle (1979) and Borg et al. (2002). For a critique of Entwistle's interpretation of this aspect of Gramsci's thought, see Giroux (1988: 196–203).

14 This theme was developed at length in Gramsci's critique of Nikolai Bukharin's *Theory of Historical Materialism: A Popular Manual of Marxist Sociology*. See Gramsci (1971: 419–472). See also Finocchiaro (1988: 68–122) and Thomas (2010: 250–255).

15 Common sense is a key concept in Gramsci's thought and has been widely discussed. See for example: Crehan (2002: 110–114); Fulton (1987: 203); Liguori (2009); Thomas (2010: esp. 16 note 61); Watkins (2011).

16 See Crehan (2002: 105–110) for a more detailed discussion of Gramsci's views on folklore.

3 Myth, Religion, and the Intellectuals

Throughout his reflections on "the question of religion or worldview," Gramsci stressed the quasi-religious role played by political parties in the intellectual and moral life of the modern world.

> One should stress the importance and significance which, in the modern world, political parties have in the elaboration and diffusion of conceptions of the world, because essentially what they do is to work out the ethics and the politics corresponding to these conceptions and act as it were as their historical "laboratory." ... For this reason one can say that the parties are the elaborators of new integral and totalitarian intelligentsias and the crucibles where the unification of theory and practice, understood as a real historical process, takes place.
>
> (Gramsci 1971: 335)[1]

While churches and religious communities had traditionally played the leading role in articulating and disseminating conceptions of the world and corresponding norms of life, political parties had come to play a comparable role in the modern world. Indeed, Gramsci observed that nowadays religious movements themselves are as likely to take the form of political parties as they are to create religious orders or other more traditional institutional forms. In this connection he noted that Modernism, one of the most important movements within contemporary Catholicism, issued not in the establishment of a new religious order but rather in the establishment of a new political party, namely, Christian Democracy (Gramsci 1971: 332).

With respect to Marxism, Gramsci described the political party as the "collective intellectual" of the revolutionary movement. He regarded the party not as the repository of "scientific truth," but rather as the vehicle for a new "intellectual–moral" worldview and as the institutional embodiment of a "national–popular collective will" (Boggs 1976: 76–77). It was in connection with the problem of how it might be possible for Marxism to unite disparate groups in a mass social movement devoted to a thoroughgoing transformation of society that Gramsci turned his attention to the lessons that could be learned from "the fortunes of religions and churches" (Gramsci 1971: 340).

The Mythic Dimension of Modern Politics

The model for Gramsci's understanding of the modern political party was Machiavelli's *The Prince*. Despite the fact that Gramsci himself always sought to emphasize the continuity between his own thinking and that of Lenin, his reflections on the nature and tasks of the revolutionary political party actually owe as much to Machiavelli's theory of the art of statecraft as they do to the Bolshevik leader's theory of the revolutionary vanguard (see Fontana 1993).

While in prison, Gramsci was preoccupied with plans for a book on the nature and tasks of the Communist Party, "a book which would derive from Marxist doctrines an articulated system of contemporary politics of the '*Prince*' type" (Gramsci 1971: 123). His writings on the Communist Party aim to define what type of political party could play the role of a "Modern Prince" (editors in Gramsci 1971: 123). According to Gramsci, what was most instructive about *The Prince* was its "mythic" form.

> The basic thing about *The Prince* is that it is not a systematic treatment, but a "live" work, in which political ideology and political science are fused in the dramatic form of a "myth". Before Machiavelli, political science had taken the form either of the Utopia or of the scholarly treatise. Machiavelli, combining the two, gave imaginative and artistic form to his conception by embodying the doctrinal, rational element in the person of a *condottiere*, who represents plastically and "anthropomorphically" the symbol of the "collective will".
>
> (Gramsci 1971: 125)

By representing the political process in terms of the qualities, characteristics, and duties of a concrete individual, Machiavelli was able to stimulate "the artistic imagination ... and [give] political passions a more concrete form" (Gramsci 1971: 125).

In the modern epoch, however, it is no longer possible to conceive of the "Prince" as an actual person. The political party has taken the place of the individual hero (Gramsci 1971: 147).

> The modern prince, the myth-prince, cannot be a real person, a concrete individual. It can only be an organism, a complex element of society in which a collective will, which has already been recognised and has to some extent asserted itself in action, begins to take concrete form. History has already provided this organism, and it is the political party— the first cell in which there come together germs of a collective will tending to become universal and total.
>
> (Gramsci 1971: 129)

Gramsci viewed Machiavelli's masterpiece

> as an historical exemplification of the Sorelian myth—i.e. of a political ideology expressed neither in the form of a cold utopia nor as learned theorising, but rather by a creation of concrete fantasy which acts on a dispersed and shattered people to arouse and organise its collective will.
>
> (Gramsci 1971: 125–126)

Georges Sorel (1847–1922) is best known for his *Reflections on Violence* (1908) in which he developed the idea that the central tenants of revolutionary socialism are best regarded as "myths" capable of inspiring the working class to action (Jennings 1991: 509). According to Sorel, myths "enclose within them all the strongest inclinations of a people, of a party, or of a class." He contrasts myth in this sense with utopias "which present a deceptive mirage of the future to the people" (Sorel cited by the editors in Gramsci 1971: 126).

For Sorel, the most powerful contemporary myth was that of the General Strike, "The myth in which Socialism is wholly comprised, i.e. a body of images capable of evoking instinctively all the sentiments which correspond to the different manifestations of the war undertaken by Socialism against modern society" (Sorel cited by the editors in Gramsci 1971: 126). According to Sorel, the significance of the idea of the General Strike is that it brings to light the "cleavage" that exists between antagonistic classes in modern societies. The General Strike "destroys all the theoretical consequences of every possible social policy; its partisans look upon even the most popular reforms as having a middle-class character; so far as they are concerned, nothing can weaken the fundamental opposition of the class war" (Sorel cited by the editors in Gramsci 1971: 126). The role of violence in the class struggle is "to maintain in the minds of the proletariat this idea of cleavage without which Socialism cannot fulfil its historical role" (cited by the editors in Gramsci 1971: 126; see Sorel 1950: 124–126, 133–135, 186).

Gramsci shared Sorel's view that socialism must be understood as a total social praxis that would influence every aspect of the lives of its adherents. Its goal was to bring about a cultural revolution comparable in scope and influence to the revolution that had been brought about by primitive Christianity and by the French Revolution. The initial stage of such a cultural revolution would thus have to involve a thoroughgoing critique of bourgeois and traditional religious myths and prejudices and the creation of a culture based for the first time on truly universal spiritual values (Kolakowski 2005: 980–981).

However, the problem with Sorel's conception of myth was that it failed to appreciate the importance of the planned and conscious element of revolutionary struggle, and it failed to attend to the creative dimension of the struggle for hegemony (Boggs 1976: 108). This was due in large part to the fact that "Sorel never advanced from his conception of ideology-as-myth to an understanding of the political party, but stopped short at the idea of the trade union" (Gramsci 1971: 127). By focusing exclusively on the *expression* of a collective will in the form of a general strike, Sorel failed to see the need for the *organization* of the collective will by the political party. Moreover, the General Strike itself is essentially "a 'passive activity' ... of a negative and preliminary kind ... which does not envision an 'active and constructive' phase of its own" (Gramsci 1971: 127). The lack of a constructive and directive dimension made this an inadequate view of revolutionary activity. "The outcome was left to the intervention of the irrational, to chance (in the Bergsonian sense of '*elan vital*') or to 'spontaneity'" (Gramsci 1971: 127).

> How could an instrument conceivably be effective if, as in Sorel's vision of things, it leaves the collective will in the primitive and elementary phase of its mere formation, by differentiation ("cleavage")— even when this differentiation is violent, that is to say destroys existing moral and juridical relations? Will not that collective will, with so rudimentary a formation, at once cease to exist, scattering into an infinity of individual wills which in the positive phase then follow separate and conflicting paths? Quite apart from the fact that destruction and negation cannot exist without an implicit construction and affirmation—this not in a "metaphysical" sense but in practice, i.e. politically, as party programme. In Sorel's case it is clear that behind the spontaneity there lies a purely mechanistic assumption, behind the liberty (will—life-force) a maximum of determinism, behind the idealism an absolute materialism.
>
> (Gramsci 1971: 128–129)[2]

The inadequacy of the Sorelian conception of myth was manifest above all "in its aversion (which takes the emotional form of an ethical repugnance) for the Jacobins, who were certainly a 'categorical embodiment' of Machiavelli's Prince" (Gramsci 1971: 130; see also Gramsci 1995: 459). As explained by Quinton Hoare and Geoffrey Nowell Smith, the translators and editors of *Selections from the Prison Notebooks*, "the concept of 'Jacobinism' is perhaps that which establishes most succinctly the unifying thread which links all of Gramsci's prison writing on history and on politics."

> [According to Gramsci] Machiavelli was a "precocious Jacobin"; Mazzini and his followers failed to be the "Jacobins" of the Risorgimento; the "Modern Prince"—i.e. the communist party—must organise and express a national–popular collective will, in other words, must be a "Jacobin" force, binding the peasants beneath the hegemony of the proletariat, and rejecting all forms of economism, syndicalism, spontaneism. What has characterised Italian history hitherto is the fact that "an effective Jacobin force was always missing".
>
> (editors in Gramsci 1971: 123)

The concept of "Jacobinism" is derived from the type of leadership exercised by the radical bourgeoisie during the French Revolution, a group that has been described as "the first unmistakably modern revolutionary community in the West" (Nisbet 1973: 266). The Jacobins began as a political club formed by a few radical deputies attending the meeting of the Estates General in 1789. They took their name from the colloquial term for the church of St. Jacques, the Dominican monastery in which they held their first meetings. Initially centered in Paris and overwhelmingly middle class in origin, the movement quickly spread throughout France in the form of clubs, and its principles were eventually adopted by many self-declared working- and lower-class movements. This success in attracting a broad-based constituency, which encompassed not only the radical elements of the bourgeoisie but also the working class and sectors of the peasantry, was essential to the success of the Jacobins (Nisbet 1973: 266–267).

By Gramsci's time, the concept of Jacobinism had become quite ambiguous, taking on a variety of meanings and political connotations. As Gramsci himself explains,

> The term "Jacobin" has ended up by taking on two meanings: there is the literal meaning, characterised historically, of a particular party in the French Revolution, which conceived of the development of French life in a particular way with a particular programme, on the basis of particular social forces; and there are also the particular methods of party and government activity which they displayed, characterised by extreme energy, decisiveness and resolution, dependent on a fanatical belief in the virtue of that programme and those methods. In political language the two aspects of Jacobinism were split, and the term "Jacobin" came to be used for a politician who was energetic, resolute and fanatical, because fanatically convinced of the thaumaturgical virtues of his ideas, whatever they might be. This definition stressed the destructive elements derived from hatred of rivals and enemies, more than the constructive one derived from having made the demands of the popular masses one's own; the sectarian element of the clique, of the small group, of unrestrained individualism, more than the national political element.
>
> (Gramsci 1971: 65–66)

This ambiguity attaching to the concept of Jacobinism was reflected over the course of Gramsci's own career. In his early writings, the term had negative connotations of sectarian, mystical, abstract, and elitist. But later, in the *Prison Notebooks*, the term is re-valued and acquires a much more positive meaning (Forgacs 1988: 426).

What most impressed Gramsci about the Jacobins was their ability to unite intellectuals and masses, workers and peasants, the city and the countryside within a single national–popular alliance. In Gramsci's mature writings, the concept of Jacobinism thus came to designate the ability of a social group to overcome a narrowly self-interested or "economic-corporate" conception of itself in order to form more expansive and universalizing alliances with other social groups whose interests could be shown as coinciding with those of the hegemonic class (editors in Gramsci 1971: 123; Forgacs 1988: 426; Sassoon 1982a: 14–15).

Gramsci regarded Machiavelli as a forerunner of the historical Jacobins insofar as he did not merely desire the national unification of Italy in the abstract, but rather had a concrete political program to accomplish this goal. His "precocious Jacobinism" was revealed by his intention to bring the great mass of peasant farmers into political life through the institution of a citizen militia (Gramsci 1971: 123–124).

> Any formation of a national–popular collective will is impossible, unless the great mass of peasant farmers bursts *simultaneously* into political life. That was Machiavelli's intention through the reform of the militia, and it was achieved by the Jacobins in the French Revolution. That Machiavelli understood it reveals a precocious Jacobinism that is the (more or less fertile) germ of his conception of national revolution. All history from 1815 onwards shows the effort of the traditional classes to prevent the formation of a collective will of this kind, and to maintain "economic–corporate" power in an international system of passive equilibrium.
>
> (Gramsci 1971: 132)

Interestingly enough, Gramsci also viewed the Protestant Reformation as something of a Jacobin force insofar as it too had embodied a genuinely national–popular movement, unlike the Italian Renaissance, which had remained restricted to an urban and cosmopolitan elite.

However, Machiavelli and the Protestant Reformation were not simply precursors of the "historical" Jacobins of the French Revolution. They were also precursors of the "modern" Jacobins, namely the Communists, whose task it now was to forge a national–popular alliance between the workers and the peasants, the intellectuals and the masses, the city and the countryside. By identifying the Communists with Jacobinism, Gramsci was developing a theme already touched on by Lenin (editors in Gramsci 1971: 124). In *Two Tactics of Social Democracy* (1905), Lenin had called the Bolsheviks the "Jacobins of contemporary Social Democracy" whose slogan is "the revolutionary–democratic dictatorship of the proletariat and peasantry" (Forgacs 1988: 426). In 1917 Lenin wrote that

> "Jacobinism" in Europe or on the boundary line between Europe and Asia in the twentieth century would be the rule of the revolutionary class, of the proletariat, which, supported by the peasant poor and taking advantage of the existing material basis for advancing to socialism, could not only provide all the great, ineradicable, unforgettable things provided

by the Jacobins in the eighteenth century, but bring about a lasting worldwide victory for the working people.

(Lenin cited by the editors in Gramsci 1971: 124; Forgacs 1988: 426)

Just as in the French Revolution, where the radical bourgeoisie during the phase of Jacobin domination had become hegemonic by universalizing and expanding its class interests in such a way as to incorporate those of the urban artisans and the peasantry, so also the proletariat would have to repeat the same process in Italy (Forgacs 1984: 87–88).

It was largely in connection with this question of how socialism might succeed in creating such a mass social movement capable of uniting disparate groups in the pursuit of a common historical project that Gramsci turned his attention to the history of Christianity and to the ethical–political role of intellectuals.

Religion and the Intellectuals

For Gramsci, the ideological and ethical distance between intellectuals and masses was a universal problem that manifested itself in a particularly striking way in the history of religions.

> In both India and China the enormous gap separating intellectuals and people is manifested also in the religious field. The problem of different beliefs and of different ways of conceiving and practising the same religion among the various strata of society, but particularly as between clergy, intellectuals and people, needs to be studied in general, since it occurs everywhere to a certain degree; but it is in the countries of East Asia that it reaches its most extreme form. In Protestant countries the difference is relatively slight (the proliferation of sects is connected with the need for a perfect suture between intellectuals and people, with the result that all the crudity of the effective conceptions of the popular masses is reproduced in the higher organisational sphere). It is more noteworthy in Catholic countries, but its extent varies. It is less in the Catholic parts of Germany and in France; rather greater in Italy, particularly in the South and in the islands; and very great indeed in the Iberian peninsula and in the countries of Latin America. The phenomenon increases in scale in Orthodox countries where it becomes necessary to speak of three degrees of the same religion: that of the higher clergy and the monks, that of the secular clergy and that of the people. It reaches a level of absurdity in East Asia, where the religion of the people often has nothing whatever to do with that of books, although the two are called by the same name.
>
> (Gramsci 1971: 23)

In the face of this disparity between intellectual and popular expressions of religious thought and practice, Gramsci concluded that Marxism, no less than traditional religions, must address two basic challenges (Bellah 1980: 89). In the first place, it must be able to provide new forms of consciousness that are appropriate for new stages of social development. Here Gramsci believed that Christianity had benefited greatly from remarkable intellectuals who knew precisely how to translate the Christian conception of the world into a practical form of consciousness and conduct. He cited St. Paul as having played a determinative role in this respect. Paul's achievement was to have elaborated a practical moral and political attitude that took account of the concrete situation of the epoch in such a way as to advance the Christian conception of the world in its competition with contemporary ideological adversaries. In short, Gramsci saw Paul as the architect of a revolutionary strategy for the spread and eventual triumph of Christianity (Portelli 1974: 57).

In this connection, Gramsci drew a comparison between the relationship of Lenin to Marx and that of Paul to Jesus. While Marx was responsible for the intellectual initiation of a new historical epoch, Lenin was responsible for the translation of this conception of the world into action. Likewise the relationship between Jesus and Paul.

> Christ—*Weltanschauung*—, and St. Paul—organiser, action, expansion of the *Weltanschauung*—are both necessary to the same degree and therefore of the same historical stature. Christianity could be called historically "Christianity–Paulinism", and this would indeed be a more exact title. (It is only the belief in the divinity of Christ which has prevented this from happening, but the belief is itself an historical and not a theoretical element.)
> (Gramsci 1971: 382; see also Portelli 1974: 56–57
> and McLellan 1987: 117)

The second major challenge facing any religion or worldview was to provide the intellectual and moral integration necessary for the formation and maintenance of society.

> [T]he fundamental problem facing any conception of the world, any philosophy which has become a cultural movement, a "religion", a "faith", any that has produced a form of practical activity or will ... is that of preserving the ideological unity of the entire social bloc which that ideology serves to cement and unify.
> (Gramsci 1971: 328)

Gramsci was impressed by the fact that religions must constantly struggle against centrifugal tendencies that regularly appear in their midst. He was especially interested in the efforts of the Catholic Church to manage these tensions and to maintain a semblance of unity.

> The strength of religions, and of the Catholic church in particular, has lain, and still lies, in the fact that they feel very strongly the need for the

doctrinal unity of the whole mass of the faithful and strive to insure that the higher intellectual stratum does not get separated from the lower. The Roman church has always been the most vigorous in the struggle to prevent the "official" formation of two religions, one for the "intellectuals" and one for the "simple souls".

(Gramsci 1971: 328)

Ultimately, however, Gramsci argued that the unity maintained by the Church was only superficial at best. Despite some appearances to the contrary, there remained fundamental divisions within the community of the faithful.

Every religion, even Catholicism (indeed Catholicism more than any, precisely because of its efforts to retain a "surface" unity and avoid splintering into national churches and social stratifications), is in reality a multiplicity of distinct and often contradictory religions: there is one Catholicism for the peasants, one for the *petit-bourgeois* and town workers, one for women, and one for intellectuals which is itself variegated and disconnected.

(Gramsci 1971: 420)

In the past, such division in the community of the faithful had often been "healed by strong mass movements which led to, or were absorbed in, the creation of new religious orders centered on strong personalities (St. Dominic, St. Francis)" (Gramsci 1971: 331).[3]

The popular classes gave birth to a long series of movements that sought to restore the original popular and egalitarian character of the Christian tradition (Mansueto 1988: 273). As Gramsci wrote, "Many heretical movements were manifestations of popular forces aiming to reform the Church and bring it closer to the people by exalting them" (1971: 397). Such groups as the Valdese, the Joachites, the Franciscans, and the mendicant orders generally all sought, in their own ways, to break the alliance of altar and sword and to purify Christian theology of feudal accretions (Mansueto 1988: 273).

The heretical movements of the Middle Ages were a simultaneous reaction against the politicking of the Church and the scholastic philosophy which expressed this. They were based on social conflicts determined by the birth of the Communes, and represented a split between masses and intellectuals within the Church. This split was "stitched over" by the birth of popular religious movements subsequently reabsorbed by the Church through the formation of the mendicant orders and a new religious unity.

(Gramsci 1971: 331)

As Anthony Mansueto has observed, Gramsci seems to suggest that these movements were defeated not because the material conditions for communism were lacking, as Engels and Kautsky had argued, but rather because they all failed to develop an effective strategy for hegemony. They were unsuccessful in uniting all of the popular classes of the city and the countryside into a single revolutionary Christian bloc capable of breaking the hold of feudalism and opening up the road to a classless and communal social order.

> Some, like the Valdese and the Franciscan Spirituals erred to the "left," becoming revolutionary sects. Others, such as the main body of the Franciscan order and the mendicant tradition generally erred to the "right," becoming reabsorbed into the Church and the cultural milieu of the times.
>
> (Mansueto 1988: 273)

But while the re-incorporation of popular movements back into the Church had been possible in the thirteenth century, it was no longer possible in the sixteenth. "Thus it was that the very religious orders founded to contain religious opposition in the high Middle Ages provided the heretical leaders of the sixteenth century—for example, Savonarola from the Dominicans, Luther from the Augustinians" (McLellan 1987: 119). Gramsci thus extended his analysis of the growing rupture between the popular classes and the intellectual elite of the Church hierarchy to an interpretation of the three great "bourgeois" revolutions: the Lutheran Reformation; the English Revolution and Calvinism; and the French Revolution (Portelli 1974: 96).

Both the medieval heresies and the Reformation involved a protest against the corruptions of feudal Catholicism and a call for a return to the scriptural purity of Christianity's origins. In the case of the medieval heresies, this call emanated for the most part from subordinate groups and represented a revolt of the masses against the intellectuals and the Church hierarchy. But it remained a revolt carried out in the name of ideology. The struggle remained situated within the existing ideological and intellectual framework, and the subordinate groups were limited to demanding an improvement of the hegemonic system already in place. Gramsci suggests that this type of heresy was increasingly manifest in both Christian and Muslim countries during the declining years of the feudal system (Portelli 1974: 94).

But with the Lutheran Reformation and the English Revolution, the theme of a "return to origins" became intertwined with a strong national sentiment. This new type of heresy moved beyond traditional ideological bounds by placing national–popular aspirations and a protest against the theocratic universalism of Rome at its center. Indeed, the "return to origins" theme eventually disappeared altogether in later revolutions as nationalism itself increasingly became the modern form of religious heresy (Portelli 1974: 94; Gramsci 1995: 134).

The hegemonic structure of medieval Christendom had been based on the ideological control of the masses by a centralized body of religious intellectuals and their characteristically cosmopolitan outlook. With the birth and development of Catholicism "the ecclesiastical organisation ... for many centuries absorbs the major part of intellectual activities and exercises a monopoly of cultural direction with penal sanctions against anyone who attempted to oppose or even evade the monopoly" (Gramsci 1971: 17; Fulton 1987: 209–210).

What Luther, Calvin, and the other reformers did was to split off the caste of religious intellectuals from the people precisely on the issue of bureaucratic and ideological centralization, thus breaking the hegemonic power of the religious ideology. Consequently, the centralizing authority principle of the hegemonic structure was itself destroyed. Once the "cosmopolitical" center of medieval Christendom was displaced, the countervailing tendencies which had previously irrupted in mystical–pacifist movements and other local and popularly based religious–political movements violently arose.[4] The very procedure of bringing God back to the people, by circumventing the language of the clerical caste and using the vernacular language, expressed this tendency. The ethical–political significance of the Reformation thus consisted above all in its challenge to the cosmopolitan or "cosmopolitical" structure of medieval Church hegemony. "The great heresy [of the Reformation] ... was the 'national feeling' directed against theocratic cosmopolitanism" (Gramsci cited in Fulton 1987: 210; see Gramsci 1995: 134).[5]

Gramsci contrasted this *nationalistic* and *popular* character of the Reformation with the *cosmopolitanism* and *elitism* of the Italian Renaissance. In the two centuries preceding the Reformation, Italy's relatively developed economy had nourished a thriving cultural, social, and political life, but it was almost totally divorced from the day to day existence of the general population (McLellan 1987: 119). It was mainly limited to a "restricted intellectual aristocracy," or "courtly circles" in Croce's words. The ideological forces set in motion by the Renaissance, though powerful, were self-contained and did not have the same wide ranging historical and political significance that the Reformation had (Boggs 1976: 49).

> Politically domination was in the hands of an aristocracy composed largely of self-made men, gathered in the courts of the nobility, and protected by bands of mercenaries: it produced the culture of the sixteenth century and helped the arts, but was politically limited and ended up under foreign domination.
>
> (Gramsci cited in McLellan 1987: 120)

The Lutheran Reformation, by contrast, was initially very backward in the area of high culture. This was attributed by Gramsci to the Reformation's character as a popular movement born by "the German people itself in its totality, as undifferentiated mass, not the intellectuals" (Gramsci 1971: 397).

> A great movement of intellectual and moral regeneration insofar as it is embodied in large popular masses, as was the case with Lutheranism,

assumes initially vulgar and even superstitious forms; this was inevitable simply because it was not a small aristocracy of great intellectuals but the German people who were the protagonists and standard-bearers of the Reformation.

(Gramsci cited in McLellan 1987: 121)

Despite this cultural backwardness in its early stages, however, the Reformation was ultimately of far greater historical and political significance than was the Renaissance, because it was not restricted to an intellectual elite. As a mass movement, it served as the vehicle for the thoroughgoing intellectual and moral transformation of the countries to which it spread.

> The Lutheran Reformation and Calvinism created a vast national–popular movement through which their influence spread: only in later periods did they create a higher culture. The Italian reformers were infertile of any major historical success. It is true that even the Reformation, in its higher phase, necessarily adopted the style of the Renaissance and as such spread even in non-protestant countries where the movement had not had a popular incubation. But the phase of popular development enabled the protestant countries to resist the crusade of the Catholic armies tenaciously and victoriously. Thus there was born the German nation as one of the most vigorous in modern Europe.
>
> (Gramsci 1971: 394)

Gramsci extended these same lines of analysis to the French Revolution, which he described as the "liberal-bourgeois reformation." In contrast to many other commentators, including Engels, Gramsci maintained that in its early phases the French Revolution was not an essentially anti-religious event. Rather, it is more appropriately viewed as an integral stage in the protracted struggle of the Reformation (Mansueto 1988: 273; Fulton 1987: 211).

> France was lacerated by the wars of religion leading to an apparent victory of Catholicism, but it experienced a great popular reformation in the eighteenth century with the Enlightenment, Voltairianism and the Encyclopaedia. This reformation preceded and accompanied the Revolution of 1789. It really was a matter here of a great intellectual and moral reformation of the French people, more complete than the German Lutheran Reformation, because it also embraced the great peasant masses in the countryside and had a distinct secular basis and attempted to replace religion with a completely secular ideology represented by the national and patriotic bond.
>
> (Gramsci 1971: 394–395)

According to Gramsci, the Jacobins succeeded in large part because they were able to present the Revolution as the defense and ultimate realization of the ideals of liberty, equality, and fraternity—ideals that were deeply rooted in the Christian tradition (Mansueto 1988: 273).

> Otherwise adherence to the new ideals and revolutionary politics of the Jacobins against the clergy by a population which was almost certainly still profoundly Catholic and religious would be inexplicable.
>
> (Gramsci cited in Mansueto 1988: 274)

The Revolution was anti-clerical to be sure, but not thereby anti-Christian or anti-religious (Fulton 1987: 211).

> One could perhaps say that the "Church" as a community of the faithful preserved and developed specific political–moral principles in opposition to the Church as a clerical organization. One can say this even of the French Revolution, whose principles are proper to the community of the faithful over and against the clergy, which is of a feudal order, allied to the king and the nobles. For this reason, many Catholics consider the French Revolution more of a schism than a heresy, that is a split between pastor and flock, similar to the Reformation, but historically more mature because occurring on the field of anti-clericalism; not priests against priests, but believers and un believers against priests.
>
> (Gramsci cited in Fulton 1987: 211)

The increasingly secular tone that eventually came to characterize French intellectual life was attributed by Gramsci in large part to the Church's efforts to maintain its monopoly in the ideological field. In order to combat more effectively the Church's ideological monopoly, the new "active conception of the world" of the Enlightenment and the revolution took on a non- or anti-religious flavor, combining the secular philosophy of the eighteenth century *philosophes* with a national–popular movement freed from the religious underpinnings of the Reformation (Fulton 1987: 211).

Meanwhile, in Italy, the Church remained part of the institutional status quo, a privileged bastion of economic wealth and social status. With the Counter-Reformation, the Catholic Church had assumed an increasingly authoritarian and disciplinary role, which had the effect of further severing the link between the masses and the intellectuals in the Church hierarchy (McLellan 1987: 121).

> But the Counter-Reformation has rendered sterile this upsurge of popular forces [that occurred in connection with the Reformation]. The Society of Jesus is the last of the great religious orders. Its origins were reactionary and authoritarian, and its character repressive and "diplomatic". Its birth marked the hardening of the Catholic organism.
>
> (Gramsci 1971: 332)

Gramsci identifies this turn of events as "the point of the breakdown between democracy and the church" (Gramsci cited in Fulton, 1987: 210). He saw evidence for this judgment in the fact that Jansenism, one of the few religious movements produced by the Counter-Reformation, was not a mass movement and did not issue in the establishment of a new religious order (Portelli 1974: 109; McLellan 1987: 121). Those new religious orders that did emerge in this period, foremost among them the Jesuits, were viewed by Gramsci not as genuine religious movements at all but rather as disciplinary arms of the papacy (Fulton 1987: 210–211).

> New orders which have grown up since then have very little religious significance but a great "disciplinary" significance for the mass of the faithful. They are, or have become, ramifications and tentacles of the Society of Jesus, instruments of "resistance" to preserve political positions that have been gained, not forces of renovation and development. Catholicism has become "Jesuitism". Modernism has not created "religious orders", but a political party—Christian Democracy.
>
> (Gramsci 1971: 332)

Thus, even in Catholic countries, the hegemony of the medieval feudal bloc was destroyed. No longer able to assert control over the mass of the population in Southern Europe primarily through ideological means, the papacy increasingly aligned itself with the coercive political power of the remaining European monarchies. The Church effectively became the ideological apparatus of the state (Fulton 1987: 210).

> With the Counter-Reformation, the papacy had changed essentially the structure of its power: it had become alienated from the masses of the people, had become an instigator of wars of extermination, and aligned itself irremediably with the ruling classes ... It is worth noting that while Bellarmine was constructing his theory of the indirect rule (*dominio*) of the church [in the state], the church was concretely destroying the conditions for any sort of rule, even indirect, by abandoning the mass of the people.
>
> (Gramsci cited in Fulton 1987: 210)[6]

As the progressive bourgeoisie gradually emerged as the ruling group in Catholic Europe outside of Italy, the Church found itself in the position of having lost its centuries-old alliance with the ruling group in society. It was left instead with its old allies, the superseded royalist faction and the peasantry (Fulton 1987: 211). Well into the modern period, the Church continued actively to resist the spread of modernism and liberalism. By stressing the "natural" God-given character of existing structures such as private property and the family, by emphasizing otherworldly rewards instead of collective action to change this world, by valorizing poverty and weakness as moral virtues and by defending the sacrosanct nature of all forms of established authority, the Church performed the concrete political role of containing and distorting popular discontent (Boggs 1976: 43).

Ultimately, of course, the Protestant reformers failed to restore the original revolutionary communitarian character of the Christian tradition. On the contrary, as Anthony Mansueto has explained, the new Protestant Christianity linked the popular religion of the peasant masses to essentially bourgeois tasks: the creation of unified national states and the development of industrial forces of production. With its emphasis on independent national churches, the Lutheran tradition bound the German masses to the task of building a German nation, which they came to see as the embodiment of their fundamentally Christian ideals. Similarly, in the English-speaking world, Calvinism bound the masses to the tremendous project of the Industrial Revolution by endowing work and economic growth with a new religious meaning. "The Protestant Reformation liberated Christianity from its feudal deformations only to recast it in a way that conformed to the needs of the rising capitalist relations of production" (Mansueto 1988: 273).[7]

It was left to Marxism, the philosophy of praxis, to continue the struggle to realize the revolutionary potential of the ideals of freedom, equality, and brotherhood and to liberate them from the ruling class political projects to which they had become attached. Indeed, Gramsci viewed the philosophy of praxis as the inheritor and most advanced expression of the historical project begun by the Reformation.

> The philosophy of praxis presupposes all this cultural past: Renaissance and Reformation, German philosophy and the French Revolution, Calvinism and English classical economics, secular liberalism and this historicism which is at the root of the whole modern conception of life. The philosophy of praxis is the crowning point of this entire movement of intellectual and moral reformation, made dialectical in the contrast between popular culture and high culture. It corresponds to the nexus Protestant Reformation plus French Revolution: it is a philosophy which is also politics, and a politics which is also philosophy.
>
> (Gramsci 1971: 395)

Yet Gramsci was dismayed by the crudeness of the forms in which Marxism had come to be preached and taught. While the Marxism of the people had become a mass social movement and strong political force in the contemporary world, it had increasingly come to rely upon a crude and simplistic combination of philosophical materialism and historical determinism at the level of ideology. At the same time, the Marxism of the intellectuals was theoretically more sophisticated, but it was politically and morally impotent as a social movement (McLellan 1987: 123). It thus appeared to Gramsci that popular Marxism was beginning to maintain with "pure" Marxism the same relationship that popular Catholicism maintained with the Catholicism of the theologians (Portelli 1974: 276).

Gramsci's problem was to prevent Marxism from degenerating into the equivalent of another popular religion while at the same time encouraging the creation of genuinely "organic" intellectuals who emerged from and remained intellectually and emotionally linked to the aspirations of the subordinate groups in society. Here again he turned his attention to the history of Christianity as a key for understanding the challenges faced by this twentieth-century movement for intellectual and moral reformation.

Marxism and the Intellectuals

The diffusion of Marxism among the masses, and the attempt to cast it in terms of common sense and the national–popular traditions of the people, created some serious problems that were not unlike those that had been encountered by Christianity in the course of its evolution. Chief among these were the degradation and vulgarization of the Marxist worldview and ethic and the emergence of a split between the Marxism of the intellectuals and that of the masses.

As it diffused and combined with the elements of common sense and popular culture, the philosophy of praxis had itself often become a form of "'prejudice' and 'superstition'" (Gramsci 1971: 396).

> The new philosophy is transformed into a form of culture which was little superior to the average popular culture (which was very low), but absolutely inadequate to combat the ideologies of the cultivated classes. Therefore, the new philosophy was never properly able to surpass the highest cultural manifestation of the epoch, classical German philosophy, nor able to sustain its own group of intellectuals attached to the new social group whose conception of the world it was.
>
> (Gramsci cited in Portelli 1974: 275)

Gramsci believed that the simplistic materialism upon which popular Marxism had come to rely was actually very closely related to popular religion and common sense. Indeed, far from being the opposite of religion as is often assumed, a certain form of naïve materialism can in fact be viewed as the direct outcome of religious superstition.

> "Politically" the materialist conception is close to the people, to "common sense". It is closely linked to many beliefs and prejudices, to almost all popular superstitions (witchcraft, spirits, etc.). This can be seen in popular Catholicism, and, even more so, in Byzantine orthodoxy. Popular religion is crassly materialistic, and yet the official religion of the intellectuals attempts to impede the formation of two distinct religions, two separate strata, so as not to become officially, as well as in reality, an ideology of restricted groups.
>
> (Gramsci 1971: 396–397)

The materialistic aspects of popular beliefs initially constituted a favorable environment for the penetration of Marxism among the subaltern classes.

> In the history of culture ... every time that there has been a flowering of popular culture because a revolutionary phase was being passed through and because the metal of a new class was being forged from the ore of the people, there has been a flowering of "materialism": conversely, at the same time traditional classes clung to philosophies of the spirit.
>
> (Gramsci 1971: 396)

But while this simple materialism might prove beneficial in the short run, it would ultimately be necessary for the philosophy of praxis to "reconstruct the synthesis of dialectical unity" between philosophical materialism and Hegelian idealism which had been the achievement of Marx.

> [T]he philosophy of praxis was born on the terrain of the highest development of culture in the first half of the nineteenth century, this culture being represented by classical German philosophy, English classical economics and French political literature and practice.
>
> (Gramsci 1971: 399)

More problematic in Gramsci's eyes was the fatalistic determinism of popular Marxism, a perspective that "appears in the role of a substitute for the Predestination or Providence of confessional religions" (Gramsci 1971: 336). Here Gramsci saw direct parallels between the evolution of early Christianity and that of twentieth-century Marxism.

Gramsci had been impressed by Georges Sorel's inquiry into primitive Christianity and by his identification of parallels between the ethic of the early Christian communities and that of the revolutionary workers' movement. As Croce explained in his *History of Europe in the Nineteenth Century*,

> Sorel assimilated socialism, as he conceived it, to primitive Christianity, assigned to it the aim of renewing society from its moral foundation, and therefore urged it to cultivate, like the first Christians, the sentiment of 'scission' from surrounding society, to avoid all relation with politicians, to shut itself up in workmen's syndicates and feed on the "myth" of the general strike.
>
> (Croce cited in Bellah 1980: 105)[8]

In his early writings, Gramsci followed Sorel's lead by viewing Christianity as an example of a thoroughgoing total revolution of the sort that socialism also sought to bring about. In a 1920 article for *L'Ordine Nuovo* (*The New Order*), Gramsci wrote that "Christianity represents a revolution at the height of its development—a revolution, that is, that has gone as far as it can, as far as creating a new and original system of moral, legal, philosophical and artistic relations" (Gramsci 1994: 187).

In later writings, however, Gramsci came to regard primitive Christianity not as an example of a successful total revolution at all, but rather as an example of a "passive revolution," that is, a revolution whose ideals and values had been compromised as a result of its incorporation by ruling elites who succeeded in transforming what had originated as a subversive ideology into a legitimating ideology for the status quo. Because it did not actively seek to replace the existing social and political system, the Christian worldview ultimately became incorporated by it. Thus, while Christianity had initially emerged as a form of ideological, spiritual, and political resistance among oppressed peoples and subordinate groups, it was eventually transformed into the official worldview of the Roman Empire and ultimately became the legitimating ideology of feudalism. "Christianity has confirmed what happens in periods of restoration as opposed to periods of revolution: the attenuated and camouflaged acceptance of the principles against which the struggle had been conducted" (Gramsci cited in McLellan 1987: 118; Portelli 1974: 61).

Gramsci adopted the concept of "passive revolution" from Vincenzo Cuoco (1770–1823), who was a Neapolitan conservative thinker of great influence in the early stages of the Risorgimento (editors in Gramsci 1971: 59). Cuoco had used the term to describe the lack of mass participation and the external origins of the Neapolitan revolution of 1799. Subsequently, under the influence of Edmund Burke's and Joseph de Maistre's writings, Cuoco came to advocate "passive revolution" as a strategic alternative to the French model where the Jacobin revolutionary strategy depended upon the participation of the popular masses (editors in Gramsci 1971: 46, 59). Gramsci uses the expression in two distinguishable ways: firstly, in something close to Cuoco's original sense, as a revolution without mass participation and due in large part to outside forces (for example, the "external" roles played by France and Austria in the Italian Risorgimento), and, secondly, "as a 'molecular' social transformation which takes place as it were beneath the surface of society, in situations where the progressive class cannot advance openly" (editors in Gramsci 1971: 46).

At the most general level, the term "passive revolution" refers to any historical situation in which a new political formation comes to power without a fundamental reordering of social relations (Forgacs 1988: 428). It is a situation that Gramsci describes "as 'revolution' without a 'revolution', or as 'passive revolution' to use an expression of Cuoco's in a slightly different sense from that which Cuoco intended" (Gramsci 1971: 59). A passive revolution is characterized by the absence of determined struggle against the old social structure and by the compromise solution, or the "revolution–restoration," that results (Portelli 1974: 58). Gramsci believed that the Risorgimento, the movements of the liberal bourgeoisie in post-1815 Restoration France, Italian Fascism, and "the development of Christianity within the bosom of the Roman Empire" all bore at least some of the characteristics of a "passive revolution" (Gramsci 1971: 107, 106–120).

In attempting to explain Christianity's failure to concretely realize its egalitarian and communal ideals, Engels and Kautsky had each followed along orthodox Marxist lines in stressing the economic factors involved. The Christian project was doomed to fail because the low level of productive forces made communism impossible at that time in history (Mansueto 1988: 272). As we have seen, Gramsci did not deny the significance of economic factors for explanations of social and historical developments, but he thought that such explanations were rarely sufficient by themselves. Thus while Gramsci entirely agreed that the original ethical–political goals of Christianity had not been successfully realized, he attributed this failure not so much to the undeveloped level of productive forces as to the passive ideological and political character that ultimately allowed Christianity to be incorporated and transformed by the ruling bloc.

According to Gramsci, there were basically two factors that helped to account for the passive character of early Christianity: its fatalistic determinism at the level of ideology along with a complete lack of a political–military dimension (Portelli 1974: 58). Implicit in early Christianity's doctrines of grace and providence and in the notion of an egalitarian resurrection was a fatalistic determinism that Gramsci viewed as having played a morally and politically ambiguous role. Initially it had constituted a formidable force of spiritual resistance to oppression.

> When you don't have the initiative in the struggle and the struggle itself comes eventually to be identified with a series of defeats, mechanical determinism becomes a tremendous force of moral resistance, of cohesion and of patient and obstinate perseverance. "I have been defeated for the moment, but the tide of history is working for me in the long term." Real will takes on the garments of an act of faith in a certain rationality of history and in a primitive and empirical form of impassioned finalism which appears in the role of a substitute for the Predestination or Providence of confessional religions.
>
> (Gramsci 1971: 336)

Gramsci speculated further about the extent to which such a deterministic ideology and its characteristic form of political expression—non-violent resistance—is typical of situations where there is a sense of material and military impotence combined with a sense of spiritual and cultural superiority.

> [Fatalism and non-violent resistance are typical in] Countries of ancient civilization, disarmed and technically (militarily) inferior, dominated by technologically developed countries (the Romans having developed governmental and military technology). The fact that a multitude of men who believe themselves to be civilized are dominated by a few men

who are considered less civilized but materially invincible, accounts for the relationship between primitive Christianity and Gandhism. The consciousness of material powerlessness of a great mass against a handful of oppressors leads to the exaltation of purely spiritual values, to passivity, to non-[violent] resistance, to non-cooperation which is however in fact a diluted and painful form of resistance, the cushion against the weight of oppression.

(Gramsci cited in Portelli 1974: 59–60; Gramsci 1995: 119)

As this passage indicates, Gramsci saw a parallel between the circumstances out of which primitive Christian ideology had arisen and those out of which the ideologies of Gandhi and also Tolstoy had arisen in his own time. Gandhism arose in an international situation characterized by an imperialistic relationship between Britain and India, which was similar in form to the relationship between Rome and Palestine in the first century CE. Tolstoyism illustrates a comparable situation within the interior of a single country, a form of domestic colonialism where a relatively small minority dominated the peasant masses, again a situation similar to that which obtained in first century Palestine. Thus in his discussion of the development of Christianity within the Roman Empire, Gramsci suggests that it is instructive to recall

Also the current phenomenon of Gandhism in India, and Tolstoy's theory of non-resistance to evil, both of which have so much in common with the first phase of Christianity (before the Edict of Milan). Gandhism and Tolstoyism are naïve theorisations of "passive revolution" with religious overtones.

(Gramsci 1971: 107)

Similarly, Gramsci attributed the strong presence of determinism in the history of Marxism to the historical circumstances of the early phases of the workers' movement. Gramsci argued that fatalistic beliefs have functioned throughout history as the ideology of dependent groups. "Indeed one should emphasise how fatalism is nothing other than the clothing worn by real and active will when in a weak position" (Gramsci 1971: 337). As it was with the early Christians, so it was also in the early days of the workers' movement. As long as a subordinate class does not possess the initiative but is restricted mainly to defensive action, it is apt to develop the compensatory idea that it is bound to triumph sooner or later because of "historical laws" and that history is "objectively" on its side.

With regard to the historical role played by the fatalistic conception of the philosophy of praxis one might perhaps prepare its funeral oration, emphasising its usefulness for a certain period of history, but precisely for that reason underlining the need to bury it with all due honours. Its role could really be compared with that of the theory of predestination and grace for the beginnings of the modern world, a theory which found its culmination in classical German philosophy and in its conception of freedom as the consciousness of necessity. It has been a replacement in the popular consciousness for the cry "'tis God's will", although even on this primitive, elementary plane it was the beginnings of a more modern and fertile conception than that contained in the expression "'tis God's will" or in the theory of grace.

(Gramsci 1971: 342)

Yet while this primitive, quasi-religious faith in predestination and providence might be necessary in the early stages of the socialist movement, it would ultimately rob the masses of all political initiative and hinder the development of an awareness among subordinate classes of their own potential to assert a collective will (Kolakowski 2005: 972). Such a conception of the world could never be successfully translated into a practical form of genuinely revolutionary activity.

That is why it is essential at all times to demonstrate the futility of mechanical determinism: for, although it is explicable as a naïve philosophy of the mass and as such, but only as such, can be an intrinsic element of strength, nevertheless when it is adopted as a thought-out and coherent philosophy on the part of intellectuals, it becomes a cause of passivity, of idiotic self-sufficiency.

(Gramsci 1971: 337)

Such a fatalistic or passive stage must be superseded by a more active and creative stage in which there is experienced "the concrete birth of a need to construct a new intellectual and moral order, that is, a new type of society, and hence the need to develop more universal concepts and more refined and decisive ideological weapons" (Gramsci 1971: 388).

Traditional and Organic Intellectuals

It was in connection with this "need to construct a new intellectual and moral order" that Gramsci developed his famous distinction between "traditional" and "organic" intellectuals. According to Gramsci, organic intellectuals arise directly from the life conditions of a fundamental social class and articulate its aspirations. Traditional intellectuals, on the other hand, are attached to institutions that had grown up under past social formations and are linked to a new ruling class as subordinate elements in its system of class rule. Thus engineers, managers, marketing and advertising specialists and the like are the organic intellectuals of the bourgeoisie, and the cadre of the communist movement the organic intellectuals of the working class. Teachers and clergy, on the other hand, are traditional intellectuals attached to feudal or early bourgeois institutions—the church and the academy—which now play only a subordinate role in the hegemonic system of the ruling class (Mansueto 1988: 271; Gramsci 1971: 5–23).

Gramsci believed that it was the task of revolutionary intellectuals to mount a thoroughgoing critique of the accepted wisdom of the established intellectual authorities and to take the lead in the creation of "an ethic in conformity with a conception of reality that has gone beyond common sense and has become, if only within narrow limits, a critical conception" (Gramsci 1971: 333–334; Boggs 1976: 77). One of the main problems confronting the philosophy of praxis was that the "great intellectuals formed on the terrain of this philosophy, beside being few in number, were not linked with the people, they did not emerge from the people, but were the expression of traditional intermediary classes, to which they returned at the great 'turning points' in history" (Gramsci 1971: 397). Gramsci compared this stage in the evolution of Marxism to the early phases of the Protestant Reformation, which had also experienced the desertion of many intellectuals, "with Erasmus at their head," as they "gave way in the face of persecution and the stake" (Gramsci 1971: 397).

> It is precisely this desertion of the intellectuals in the face of the enemy which explains the "sterility" of the Reformation in the immediate sphere of high culture, until, by a process of selection, the people, which remained faithful to the cause, produced a new group of intellectuals culminating in classical [German] philosophy.
>
> (Gramsci 1971: 397)

The fact that the philosophy of praxis had been slow in producing a higher culture did not come as a surprise to Gramsci. On the contrary, "The process of creating intellectuals is long, difficult, full of contradictions, advances and retreats, dispersals and regroupings, in which the loyalty of the masses is often sorely tried" (Gramsci 1971: 334). Gramsci believed that Marxism was still going through its "romantic period of struggle, the period of popular *Sturm und Drang*" (Gramsci 1971: 387–388), and he noted that even the French Revolution had not "had an immediate flowering of high culture, except in political science in the form of the positive science of right" (Gramsci 1971: 395). Marxist intellectuals had too often fallen prey to the traditional paradigms and conventions of intellectual discourse, often becoming elitist and even obscurantist in the process. This had created a gap between the intellectuals and the masses, which had proven to be a persistent source of tension within the international socialist movement.

This tension between the elitism and political isolation of the intellectuals on the one hand, and the anti-intellectualism and anti-Marxism of the masses on the other hand, had in fact become a recurrent theme in the Marxist theory of the first half of the twentieth century (Boggs 1976: 77). Kautsky and European Social Democracy had addressed this issue by assuming that the ideology and often the leadership for the masses of non-intellectuals would have to be provided by intellectual refugees from the bourgeoisie (editors in Gramsci 1971: 3). Lenin had contested this view by asserting that, within the revolutionary political party, "all distinctions as between workers and intellectuals ... must be obliterated" (Lenin cited by the editors in Gramsci 1971: 3–4). Nevertheless, Lenin too believed that socialist consciousness must be brought to the working class from the outside. The agency for accomplishing this task was not the traditional intelligentsia, however, but the revolutionary party itself, in which former workers and former professional intellectuals of bourgeois origin had fused into a single cohesive unit (editors in Gramsci 1971: 4).

Finally, an alternative approach to this issue was offered by such writers as Georges Sorel and Rosa Luxemburg, each of whom, in his and her own distinctive ways, advocated an approach that relied more on the capacity of the masses themselves to guide the revolutionary struggle. Through outbursts of spontaneous energy and collective actions such as general strikes and violent confrontations with the forces of the industrial establishment, the masses would bring down the existing order and play an active role in leading the process of socialist liberation. Contrary to Bolshevism, the definition and leadership of the revolutionary project would be left in the hands of the masses rather than in the hands of a highly organized nucleus of professional revolutionaries (see McLellan 2007: 49–53, 190–195).

Gramsci's concept of "organic intellectual" and his way of understanding the nature and role of the revolutionary political party provided something of a synthesis of all three of these approaches. Indeed, Gramsci's distinction between traditional and organic intellectuals was the result of his attempt to imagine a way in which intellectuals could play both a "leading" and a "representative" role in the social existence of subaltern classes (Boggs 1976: 77). Organic intellectuals do not simply describe social life from outside in accordance with scientific principles. They use the language of culture to express the real experiences and feelings that the masses cannot express for themselves. In order to understand those experiences, they must feel the same passions as the masses (Kolakowski 2005: 979).

> The popular element "feels" but does not always know or understand; the intellectual element "knows" but does not always understand and in particular does not always feel. The two extremes are therefore pedantry and philistinism on the one hand and blind passion and sectarianism on the other ... The intellectual's error consists in believing that one can know without understanding and even more without feeling and being impassioned ... that is, without feeling the elementary passions of the people, understanding them and therefore explaining and justifying them in the particular historical situation and connecting them dialectically to the laws of history and to a superior conception of the world, scientifically and coherently elaborated—i.e. knowledge. One cannot make politics-history without this passion, without this sentimental connection

between intellectuals and people–nation. In the absence of such a nexus the relations between the intellectual and the people–nation are, or are reduced to, relationships of a purely bureaucratic and formal order; the intellectuals become a caste, or a priesthood.

(Gramsci 1971: 418)

Intellectual defectors from the bourgeoisie would initially have an important role to play in the revolutionary workers' movement, but writers like Kautsky had exaggerated this factor. Long-range revolutionary transformation would depend on the emergence of "organic" intellectuals. Hence,

One of the most important characteristics of any group that is developing toward dominance is its struggle to assimilate and conquer "ideologically" the traditional intellectuals, but this assimilation and conquest is made quicker and more efficacious the more the group in question succeeds in simultaneously elaborating its own intellectuals.

(Gramsci 1971: 10; Boggs 1976: 78)

With the concept of the organic intellectual, Gramsci sought to outline an understanding of revolutionary activity that stood as an alternative to the sort of anarchistic spontaneous mass movement envisioned by Sorel or Luxemburg on the one hand, and to Lenin's elitist and authoritarian vision of the revolutionary transition on the other (Boggs 1976: 108–109). At the same time, it allowed him to preserve Leninism's emphasis on the directive and disciplinary role of the political party while balancing and combining it with Social Democracy's emphasis on the politics of mass social movements.[9]

Gramsci thus envisaged a reciprocal pedagogical relationship between the intellectuals and the masses. Socialism could never be imposed from "above" or "outside," but would have to be the self-conscious expression of the oppressed groups themselves (Boggs 1976: 79). On this view, the introduction of new ideas and values was not simply a matter of propaganda but rather a matter of integration into the fabric of proletarian culture, lifestyles, language, and traditions by revolutionaries who themselves worked and lived within the same environment. Only this could insure the reciprocal relationship between theory and practice, the intellectual and the spontaneous, the political and the social, which could lay the foundations upon which Marxism would emerge as a real counter-hegemonic force and as the first truly popular *Weltanschauung* in history (Boggs 1976: 78).

Gramsci thus dreamed of a Marxism that would be a kind of synthesis of humanism and the Reformation (Kolakowski 2005: 981). Avoiding the natural crudity of a popular worldview, it would preserve its appeal to the masses while acquiring the ability to solve complex cultural problems. It would be "a culture that … would synthesize Robespierre and Kant, politics and philosophy, into a dialectical unity within a social group, no longer merely French or German but European and world-wide" (Gramsci cited in

Kolakowski 2005: 981). Indeed, as we have seen, Gramsci construed the entire modern revolutionary process, from Luther and Calvin through Robespierre to Lenin, as a prolonged struggle to realize the egalitarian and communal ideals of the popular masses, ideals that are themselves rooted to a great extent in the worldview and ethic of primitive Christianity (Mansueto 1988). It was in this sense that Gramsci understood Marxism as the "inheritor" of the intellectual and moral revolution that was begun but never fulfilled by primitive Christianity (see Portelli 1974: 158–262).

Beyond Gramsci

There are, of course, any number of questions that can be raised about Gramsci's interpretation of the history of religion and about his comparisons of Marxism and Christianity. One of the most obvious areas in which Gramsci's account is open to dispute is his interpretation of the social origins and ethical–political character of primitive Christianity.

Like many writers before and since, Gramsci was primarily interested in early Christianity as a type of revolutionary social movement (see Bammel 1984). As we have seen, Gramsci regarded primitive Christianity as an expression of the suffering of subordinate groups in the Roman Empire and of their longing for a classless and communal social order. Arising in the dual context of Roman oppression of Palestine and of a social minority's oppression of subordinate classes within Palestine, Christianity embodied a form of spiritual resistance to domination that eventually spread among oppressed peoples throughout the Mediterranean world (Mansueto 1988: 272; Portelli 1974: 57–60).

Whether or not early Christianity can be accurately characterized as a form of social protest arising among poor and oppressed groups within the Roman Empire has been a recurrent question, not only among Marxists, but also in academic scholarship regarding the first Christians. One school of thought has argued that early Christianity was indeed a movement of and for the poor and destitute, made up largely of slaves, peasants, workers, and the dispossessed. However, an alternative school of thought claims that Christianity's primary appeal was not to the poor, but rather to socially diverse urban groups supported in communities by their most prominent members. The "sponsors" of these communities were predominantly urban "middle-status" holders who enjoyed an elevated socio-economic status at least by comparison to the numerous poor (Longenecker 2009: 38–39).[10] Scholarship remains divided on this question of the socio-economic make-up and ethical–political character of Pauline Christianity. What is clear, however, is that even if some of Gramsci's basic intuitions are eventually confirmed, his account of early Christianity and his identification of parallels between early Christianity and the modern workers' movement stand in need of considerable refinement.

The same must be said for Gramsci's interpretation of the Protestant Reformation, a topic that has been a continual source of controversy within

Marxist scholarship, not to mention academic scholarship more generally (Jones 1996; Tonkin 1996a, 1996b). As we have seen, Gramsci regarded the Protestant Reformation as a genuinely popular movement carried forward by the great masses of the German people. He found evidence for the popular character of the Reformation in the fact that its early phases were marked by an absence of traditional intellectuals and a correspondingly low level of cultural attainment. In this connection he cited Erasmus' judgment that "where Luther appears, culture dies" (Gramsci 1995: 407). For Gramsci, this exemplified the typical aristocratic refusal to participate in popular movements, an attitude analogous in many respects to that of the Italian intellectuals during the Renaissance.

As we have seen, Gramsci believed that the overriding historical and ethical–political significance of the Reformation consisted in its success at uniting the newly emergent bourgeoisie and the great masses of the German people into a "national–popular" movement directed against the theocratic cosmopolitanism of the Roman Church. By introducing the masses into the political and cultural life of Europe and thereby transforming bourgeois movements into national revolutions, the Protestant Reformation stood as an important model for the "modern popular reformation" of Marxism (Gramsci 1995: 407–408; Portelli 1974: 106; Adamson 1987/8: 327).

Gramsci's position on this issue runs contrary to mainline Marxist interpretations of the Protestant Reformation. Engels, for example, had argued that the Reformation should be viewed as a conjunction between two often contradictory and antagonistic movements: a bourgeois revolution led by the figures of Luther and Calvin on the one hand and a peasant revolt led by Thomas Müntzer on the other. According to Engels, the Protestant Reformation failed to achieve its potential as a genuinely popular revolution because Luther and the bourgeoisie ultimately allied themselves with the nobility. The peasant revolt was dispelled by force at the price of a partial return to the old order (Portelli 1974: 118–119). Thus, Engels viewed the Reformation not as a genuinely popular mass movement, but rather as an essentially bourgeois movement with Luther as the representative of the bourgeois party.[11]

Here again it must be acknowledged that Gramsci's discussions of the Reformation are often lacking in concrete detail and fail to come to terms with the historical complexity of the period, events, and figures in question. Gramsci's treatment of the Protestant Reformation is full of insights and is highly suggestive for future research into religion, nationalism, and the politics of mass social movements. But his thoughts on this topic, as on the history of religions more generally, are often highly speculative and sometimes amount to little more than intuitions and preliminary hypotheses. It is only fair to note, however, that Gramsci was himself well aware of the limitations of his investigations and very tentative about his conclusions, declaring that any adequate treatment of the religious question would depend upon a much more thorough and detailed analysis of texts than was possible for him under the prison conditions in which he was working (Portelli 1974: 65 note 5).

Far more problematic than disputes over the details of historical interpretation is Gramsci's failure to appreciate the resilience of traditional religions in the modern world. Despite his break with positivism in other respects, Gramsci's discussions of religion often reflect a residual evolutionism that is characteristic of both the liberal and the socialist heirs of the Enlightenment critique of religion. Like Croce and any number of other modern intellectuals, Gramsci believed that the passage from a superstitious and "transcendental" conception of life to a scientific, critical, and "immanentist" worldview was historically inevitable (Adamson 1987/8: 328). This, combined with his own faith in the "philosophy of praxis," seems to have blinded him to the ongoing capacity of traditional "confessional" religions to respond in creative and critical ways to the ideological and political realities of the modern and post-modern world.

It may well be true, as Gramsci predicted, that the hierarchy of the Roman Catholic Church will never cease trying to maintain centralized and authoritarian control over its intellectuals and over its "cosmopolitan" institutional structure, this despite the post-Vatican II movement of the 1960s within the national churches for decentralization and greater freedom of conscience. But it is also true that Catholicism, along with other "confessional" religious traditions, has continued to provide the ideological and institutional contexts for some of the most profound and prophetic critiques of the status quo that can be found in the contemporary world, the tradition of Papal social encyclicals and liberation theology among them. Obviously, we can only guess at how Gramsci's view of traditional religions in the modern world might have been transformed by the "Marxist–Christian" dialogues of the 1950s and 1960s or by such subsequent developments as the resurgence of religion's role in public life in what is increasingly described as a post-secular age.

In addition to his underestimation of traditional religion, Gramsci overestimated the capacity of new "secular religions" such as Marxism to fulfil people's "spiritual" needs. While acceptance of the need for a secular religious replacement for Christianity may seem closer to Durkheim than to Marx, Gramsci nonetheless agreed with Croce that one must not take away people's religion without giving them something that satisfied the same needs (Gramsci 1995: 408–410; see also Adamson 1987/8: 327–329; Reed 2012). Though Croce eventually and reluctantly had to admit, despite himself, that idealistic philosophy could not perform this role for the majority of people, Gramsci had no doubt that the philosophy of praxis could provide the foundation and content for a new and total culture. Marxism would take the place of previous worldviews, but it could only do so if people could recognize it as an expression of their own experiences. Gramsci was confident that the working class was on the way to creating its own original culture, quite different from that of the bourgeoisie or the Church. It would supplant traditional religious and bourgeois myths and prejudices and set up for the first time truly universal spiritual values (Kolakowski 2005: 981).

Today it is impossible to share Gramsci's faith in the myth of the proletariat or his confidence in the redemptive power of modern political parties and socialist politics. Indeed, as Walter Adamson has remarked, the fact that "such a world-historical vision was still plausible in the 1930s dramatizes the very great political distance we have travelled in the last half century" (1987/8: 331). Marxism itself, as other movements before it, became detached from those whose aspirations it initially sought to express. In this connection, Anthony Mansueto has argued that while Gramsci was right to regard Marxism as the product of a long historical struggle for intellectual and moral reformation, he was wrong to have viewed it as the final product or culmination of that process. On the contrary, according to Mansueto, the socialist movement historically embraced *both* the struggle of the poor and oppressed for a classless and communal social order, *and* the radical bourgeois technocratic project of rationalization, industrialization, bureaucratization, and secularization (1988: 275). Marxism, no less than the Christian tradition from which it derives so much, can be and has been mobilized by various elite strata and ruling classes as a means for exercising hegemony over the popular sectors.

> Indeed, if [Protestantism] is to be regarded as the "Christianity" of the rising bourgeoisie, and liberalism as the "Christianity" of the established bourgeoisie, ought not Marxism, in a very real sense, or at least the productivist ideology which today passes for classical Marxism be regarded as the "Christianity" of the radical bourgeois, technocratic elite which has hegemonized the international communist movement? Marxism, like other deformations of the Christian tradition, has subordinated the aspirations of the poor and oppressed for a classless and communal society to the political project of a rising elite, while drawing on those aspirations to forge among the poor a base of mass support.
> (Mansueto 1988: 275–276)

Having said all of this, however, there is much that we can still learn from Gramsci's approach to "the question of religion or worldview." Indeed, I share David McLellan's judgment when he writes that

> Gramsci's meditations on the lessons to be learned from a comparison between Marxism and Christianity remain, at least in a socio-political perspective, the foremost Marxist contribution to the study of religion. His discussions are, of necessity, frequently fragmentary and allusive: but for their sympathy, insight, and suggestiveness they are rarely equalled.
> (1987: 123)

Undoubtedly, Gramsci's single greatest contribution is to have focused our attention on the religious and ethical dimensions of the struggle for power in history and society (Fulton 1987: 21). By following this lead, it may not only be possible to shed light on the nature and function of religious–moral discourses in the lives of human communities. It may also suggest a way of relating scholarship to the great debates of our age and of gaining for the fields of religious studies and comparative religious ethics a greater degree of public relevance.

Gramsci's work generates a valuable framework for thinking about the politics of religious–moral discourses. His reformulation of the Marxist concept of ideology and his elaboration of the concept of hegemony; his definition of "religion" as a "unity of faith between a conception of the world and corresponding norm of life"; his distinction between traditional "confessional" religions and modern secular or "lay" religions and between the religions of the intellectuals and the religions of the people; his discussion of philosophy, common sense, and folklore—these are valuable conceptual resources for the development of a critical–contextual approach to the study of religion and ethics. It is to a more detailed consideration of this project that we now turn.

Notes

1 In this context, the term "totalitarian" means totalistic or comprehensive and all-encompassing (editors in Gramsci 1971: 335 note 20).
2 Gramsci states a similar criticism of Rosa Luxemburg's notion of the mass strike, describing it as "out and out historical mysticism, the awaiting of a sort of miraculous Illumination" (1971: 233). See Boggs (1976: 55–84), Femia (1981), and McLellan (2007: 205) for a general discussion of Gramsci's critique of the sort of revolutionary "spontaneism" represented by both Sorel and Luxemburg.
3 It is interesting to note here that Gramsci's interpretation of the medieval heresies and the emergence of new religious orders as a symptom of the growing rupture between the intellectual elite of the Church hierarchy and the popular masses contrasts with Engels' interpretation of these developments as proto-bourgeois movements that simply foreshadowed the Reformation. See McLellan (1987: 117–122).
4 Fulton (1987: 208) argues convincingly that the term "cosmopolitical" better captures the significance of Gramsci's argument than does the more standard "cosmopolitan."
5 It should be noted that Gramsci believed that the cosmopolitanism of feudal Catholicism was a necessary phenomenon to the extent that Christianity presented itself as a universal religion. But this tendency had been considerably reinforced by the Church's relationship with the imperial state (Portelli 1974: 61). A chief organizational consequence of the alliance between altar and sword in the later phases of the Roman Empire had been to pattern the structure of the Church on that of the imperial state. The imperial state was cosmopolitan in its ideological orientation, and, at the institutional level, it was highly centralized, hierarchical, and focused on the person of an emperor who was invested with religious attributes. This ideological orientation was reproduced in the cosmopolitanism of Catholic theology, and this institutional form was reproduced in the institution of the papacy. The Pope inherited the religious attributions of the emperor and the tradition of the imperial cult, and the cult served to cement the intellectual cosmopolitanism (Portelli 1974: 62).

> It would be interesting to see if one could uncover a line between the cult of the emperor and the position of the pope as the vicar of God on earth. It is certain that one pays to the pope divine honours and that one calls him "our father" as

one addresses God. The pope has become an amalgam of the attributes of Grand Pontiff and of those of the divinized emperor.

(Gramsci cited in Portelli 1974: 62)

The change in the condition of the social position of the intellectuals in Rome between Republican and Imperial times (a change from an aristocratic-corporate to a democratic-bureaucratic regime) is due to Caesar, who granted citizenship to doctors and to masters of the liberal arts so that they would be more willing to live in Rome and so that others should be persuaded to come there … Caesar therefore proposed: 1. to establish in Rome those intellectuals who were already there, thus creating a permanent category of intellectuals, since without their permanent residence there no cultural organisation could be created; and 2. to attract to Rome the best intellectuals from all over the Roman Empire, thus promoting centralisation on a massive scale. In this way there came into being the category of "imperial" intellectuals in Rome which was to be continued by the Catholic clergy and to leave so many traces in the history of Italian intellectuals, such as their characteristic "cosmopolitanism", up to the eighteenth century.

(Gramsci 1971: 17)

6 Robert Bellarmine (1542–1621), an influential Cardinal–theologian and Jesuit, was one of the most important figures of the Counter-Reformation. He was canonized by Pope Pius XI in 1930.

7 Gramsci's brief remarks on Calvinism are very similar to those of Max Weber, whose *The Protestant Ethic and the Spirit of Capitalism* he explicitly cites (Gramsci 1971: 338). Gramsci regarded the Calvinist doctrines of predestination and grace as "a form of worldly rationality which provided a general framework for real practical activity" (Gramsci cited in McLellan 1987: 121). "Calvinism … with its iron conception of predestination and grace … produces a vast expansion of the spirit of initiative (or becomes the form of this movement) …" (Gramsci 1971: 338). Calvinism was thus viewed as a classic example of a "transition from a conception of the world to a norm of practical conduct" and was "one of the greatest impulses to practical action in the history of the world" (Gramsci cited in McLellan 1987: 121; See also Portelli 1974: 107, and Bocock 1986: 93–102). Various forms of Calvinist Protestantism emerged as hegemonic religious ideologies in England, the Netherlands, and the United States. In accordance with the notion of predestination, earthly achievements and good deeds became a measure of religious salvation. A practical ethic based on the values of hard work, thrift, frugality, sacrifice, and self-discipline corresponded well with the demands for technological productivity and bureaucratic efficiency and provided the core moral consciousness of an emerging capitalist order. In a fascinating section of the *Prison Notebooks* titled "Americanism and Fordism," Gramsci followed along the lines of other writers, such as Werner Sombart, in observing that the Protestant ethic was more universally assimilated by the popular masses in the United States than elsewhere and in attributing this fact in large part to the absence of feudal remnants such as an established Church and to the more advanced levels of industrial development. In this same connection, he speculated that Protestantism's strong puritanical regulation of moral-personal life helped to create in the United States an historically new type of personality—a personality type so absorbed in the rationalized work process that pleasure, sensuality, and critical thinking could only be expressed in the most restrictive and often guilt-ridden manner (Boggs 1976: 43–44).

8 For a discussion of Sorel's reflections on religion and ethics see Stanley (1981, 2002: 163–218). For discussion of Sorel's shifting conceptions of "socialism" and his ambiguous relationship to Fascism see Antliff (2007).

9 Closely related to the concept of the organic intellectual is the concept of "democratic philosopher"—"the historical realisation of a new type of philosopher … in the sense that he is a philosopher convinced that his personality is not limited to himself as a

physical individual but is an active social relationship of modification of the cultural environment" (Gramsci 1971: 350; see Thomas 2010: 429–436).

10 For overviews of debates regarding the social–economic profile of the Pauline Christian communities, see Crossley (2006) and Elliott (2012).

11 It is interesting to note in passing that Gramsci, an Italian, regarded Lutheranism itself as only a very primitive stage of the new European culture that would eventually emerge as the long-term consequence of the Reformation. By contrast, Engels, a German, described Luther as a "giant of thought, of passion and of character, [a] giant of universality and erudition" (Portelli 1974: 118). For more on the controversy within Marxist scholarship on the question of whether the Reformation was a genuinely popular or a more narrowly bourgeois religious–social movement see McLellan (1987) and Tonkin (1996a).

4 World Order in a Global Age

In the remaining chapters of this book we will draw on some aspects of Gramsci's thought that shed light on the politics of religious–moral discourses. We will see that Gramsci's work provides a valuable framework for addressing questions about the relationship between religious ethics, social order, and social change as well as the relationship between religious ethics and the interests of social groups.

Religion, Ethics, and Social Order

As a first step toward addressing questions about religion and social order, it is helpful to recall the basic features of two main theoretical approaches to this topic. The first of these is typically described as a "functionalist" or "integrationist" approach. Very simply put, this approach sees "society" as an integrated system whose various parts work together so as to promote cohesiveness and maintain the continuity and equilibrium of the system as a whole. Functionalist approaches tend to stress coherence, consensus, and solidarity among society's members. They seek to examine each element of society from the point of view of its contribution to social integration.

This approach is most often affiliated with what Bruce Lincoln has described as a "romantic" understanding of the relationship between religion and society, which emphasizes religion's role in maintaining the intellectual and moral stability of social systems (2003: 77–79). This is accomplished by furnishing people with a sense of meaning, purpose, and worth; by giving them hope in the face of suffering and death; by providing a framework of values and behavioral norms that regulate social interaction; and by providing rituals through which individuals establish a sense of identity and belonging. Religious myths, doctrines, and ceremonies serve to explain the origins and justify the continued existence of the established social order. Morality provides guidelines for socially acceptable behavior and reinforces social boundaries. Religion and morality serve as a kind of "social cement" that binds society together into a unified whole.

In contrast to the functionalist approach, the standard "Marxist" approach stresses dissensus and conflict in its account of society. Some groups rule and others are ruled; society's various institutions serve the interests of those in power more than they serve the interests of society-as-a-whole. This approach emphasizes the degree to which social order is maintained as much through deception and the threat or exercise of coercion and force as it is through consensus. The "romantic" view is replaced by a "materialist" understanding of religious–moral discourses and institutions. The focus is not so much on the role of religion in the intellectual and moral integration of society-as-a-whole. Rather,

> "materialist" analysis has tended to argue that religion serves only the interests of certain privileged strata, preserving their wealth, power, and position, while actively inhibiting any threats to them. This is accomplished in a number of ways, most notably by casting the material interests of the privileged or dominant into ideological form and presenting these as eternal truths; rechanneling the discontent of subalterns into otherworldly aspirations; and, where conflict is inevitable, canalizing it into ritual forms where it can be purged and rendered harmless.
>
> (Lincoln 2003: 77)[1]

As Lincoln makes clear, despite the very significant differences between them, functionalist and Marxist approaches are similar in one important respect. They both perceive religion as fulfilling essentially the same role: providing solace for the suffering and stability for society. Religion is a matter of preserving and legitimating the status quo, of upholding the established social and moral order. Where the two approaches differ is on the value they accord this function. The "functionalists" or "romantics" stress the positive role played by religion in the intellectual and moral integration of social life. The "Marxists" or "materialists," on the other hand, focus on the role of religion in blinding people to the realities of exploitation and class domination (Lincoln 2003: 78).

It goes without saying that both of these approaches have contributed a great deal to our understanding of the role of religion and morality in the social and political lives of human communities. Yet there are problems with each of these perspectives. One problem is that neither perspective provides an adequate account of the complex *relationship* between consent *and* coercion, persuasion *and* force, which typically stands at the foundation of most forms of social order. A second problem is that both of these approaches lead to a rather one-dimensional focus on "religions of the status quo"; neither of them adequately accounts for the full range of ways in which religious–moral discourses have been and can be involved in social–political processes—not only in the reproduction of social systems and the maintenance of social order but also in the instigation and shaping of social change (Lincoln 2003, 1989).

Here is where the work of Gramsci becomes relevant. More specifically, the Gramscian concept of hegemony enables us to incorporate both the functionalist stress on social consensus and the Marxist emphasis on social conflict within a single theoretical framework. Not only does this provide the basis for a more adequate account of the relationship between religion, ethics, and social order (the subject of this chapter), but it also sets the stage for a more dynamic and differentiated way of thinking about the role of religious–moral discourses in struggles for social change (the subject of the next chapter).

Consent and Coercion

There are some striking parallels between Gramsci's discussion of hegemony and Emile Durkheim's integrationist approach to social order. Like Durkheim, and in contrast to Marx, Gramsci was preoccupied throughout his writings with the intellectual and moral bases of social solidarity and with the question of how consent is produced in different historical periods by different social groups. It was in this connection that he sought to compare the hegemonic strategies of the medieval Church and of the European bourgeoisie with that of the twentieth-century workers' movement (see Boer 2009: 215–274).

As we saw in the preceding chapter, Gramsci believed that the hegemony of medieval Christendom and of nineteenth-century liberalism had both been based upon a form of "passive" and "indirect" consent. The Church, for example, addressed the divisions within the community of the faithful "by imposing an iron discipline on the intellectuals so that they do not exceed certain limits of differentiation and so render the split catastrophic and irreparable" (Gramsci 1971: 331). As for the common people, Catholicism "tends to maintain a purely mechanical contact, an external unity based in particular on the liturgy and on a cult visually imposing to the crowd" (Gramsci 1971: 397).

By contrast, socialist hegemony would have to be rooted in the "active" and "direct" consent and participation of the masses. Gramsci claims that the philosophy of praxis seeks to maintain "a dynamic contact [with the people] and tends continually to raise new strata of the population to a higher cultural life" (1971: 397).

> The position of the philosophy of praxis is the antithesis of the Catholic. The philosophy of praxis does not tend to leave the "simple" in their primitive philosophy of common sense, but rather to lead them to a higher conception of life. If it affirms the need for contact between the intellectuals and simple it is not in order to restrict scientific activity and preserve unity at the low level of the masses, but precisely in order to construct an intellectual-moral bloc which can make politically possible the intellectual progress of the mass and not only of small intellectual groups.
>
> (Gramsci 1971: 332–333)[2]

This focus on the consensual basis of social order and upon the role of "traditional" and "secular" religions in the production of consent is what most directly links Gramsci's work with the functionalist or integrationist approach to social order.

Gramsci's notion of hegemony stresses that the establishment and maintenance of social order in most cases depends as much on the successful exercise of intellectual and moral persuasion as it does upon the exercise of coercion and force. Indeed, as we have seen, the concept of hegemony may itself be defined as intellectual and moral leadership which is based on the consent of the major groups in society. Such consent is secured by the diffusion and popularization of the worldview and ethos of the dominant social group. This moves us well beyond orthodox Marxism's tendency to dismiss the issue of consent as an artefact of bourgeois political philosophy and as nothing more than a false ideology that blinds people to the realities of exploitation and state power (Sassoon 1982c: 116).

But like Marx, and unlike Durkheim, Gramsci always assumed a conflictual view of society in which a variety of parties are locked in a struggle for wealth, influence, and power. The concept of hegemony requires us to situate any discussion of moral persuasion and consent within the context of such struggles. This attention to conflict and struggle between competing worldviews and norms is essential to a critical–contextual approach to the study of religious ethics.

While it would not be accurate to claim that Durkheim and the functionalists ignore social conflict entirely, it is true that they tend to conceptualize such conflict in terms of oppositions between the individual and the collective rather than between interest groups in a system of domination and subordination. Moreover, conflict is typically seen in terms of something pathological or as a deviation from the norm. Where conflicts do emerge, they are not viewed as a fundamental aspect of social systems, but rather as secondary or dysfunctional effects of social or economic changes that have outpaced society's ability to develop corresponding forms of moral regulation (Joseph 2003: 197). As Anthony Giddens has pointed out, when Durkheim spoke of "interests," he usually did so in the context of the push and pull of egoism versus altruism, the interests of the individual in conflict with those of the community as a whole (1978: 111–112).

> The notion that society could be conceptualized as a system of groups chronically in tension is foreign to his viewpoint, which treats societies as unified wholes (regardless of whether the basis of such unity is traced to mechanical or organic solidarity). Conflict or division of interest between groups is treated only as a phenomenon of transitional phases in social development, in which the alignment of functions is temporarily out of equilibrium.
>
> (Giddens 1978: 112)

Moreover, in Durkheim's writings, religious teachings and moral norms are generally discussed as if they were unified across a particular society and as though they were capable of only one mode of interpretation by the members of that society (Giddens 1978: 111–112). By contrast, Gramsci stresses the cultural heterogeneity that often exists within a society (sub-cultures, counter-cultures, etc.) and the political interplay between dominant and oppositional cultural expressions. His distinction between the "religion of the intellectuals" and the "religion of the people" and his discussions of the medieval heresies and the Protestant Reformation, for example, serve to illustrate how a single set of symbols and codes, such as those involved in Christian dogma, can become the subject of variant and antagonistic interpretations, likely to be tied to the struggles between divergent interest groups. Thus, in contrast to Durkheim's view that "religion is a unified system of beliefs and practices … which unite into one single moral community called a Church, all those who adhere to them" (1965: 62), Gramsci focuses our attention on the roles played by worldviews and ethics in social systems that are characterized by ongoing struggles between dominant and subordinate groups.

It is here that we can begin to appreciate Gramsci's significance for the critical–contextual study of religion and ethics. By calling our attention to conflict and struggle between competing worldviews and norms, by encompassing a focus on both consent and conflict within a single framework, the Gramscian concept of hegemony sets the theoretical context for understanding the nature and function of religious–moral discourses as "languages of persuasion," which are, along with the exercise of coercion and force, the primary means by which human communities seek to establish and maintain social order.

Like languages, conceptions of the world and norms of life must be learned. They are the product of cumulative experiences and traditions by which they are shaped and modified over time—they are historical realities that emerge, evolve, increase or decline in saliency and influence, and are modified and sometimes incorporated by other worldviews and ethics with which they come into contact (Bird 1981: 159, 163). As "languages of persuasion," moral discourses serve to communicate specific agreements, claims, and expectations in order to regulate, control, or determine human behavior. They seek to persuade people to act in expected or desired manners by using a vocabulary and rhetoric that invokes some given social agreements about conduct—agreements that are rooted in various combinations of common sense, custom, tradition, reason, and emotion (Bird 1981: 159–160). Their persuasiveness is due in large part to their ability to invoke a variety of assumptions about human nature, the world, the future, and the past as well as possible rewards and threats that help to make particular normative claims and models compelling. As languages of persuasion, religious–moral discourses perform a range of social functions. Among the most important of these are the identification and protection of social boundaries, the interpretation and regulation of social intercourse between individuals and groups, and the reinforcement of systems of social, political, and occupational identity, status, and hierarchy (Bird 1981: 175).

Yet by calling attention to the aspects of class rule that are non-coercive, Gramsci did not wish to deny that coercion and force play a decisive role in the defense of social order and in the struggle between social groups. On the contrary, the ascendency and supremacy of a hegemonic group is ultimately consolidated and guaranteed by its capacity to exercise what Gramsci described as "political–military" leadership and power (Gramsci 1971: 107, 175–185). Citing Francesco Guicciardini's claim that "two things are absolutely necessary for the life of a state: arms and religion," Gramsci writes that

> This formula of his can be translated into various other, less drastic, formulas: force and consent, coercion and persuasion, state and Church, political society and civil society, politics and morals (Croce's ethico-political history), law [*diritto*] and freedom, order and discipline, or, with an implicit judgement of a libertarian flavour, violence and fraud.
>
> (1995: 17)[3]

Under "normal" conditions, the successful exercise of hegemony will involve a minimum use of force. The supremacy of a social group or ruling bloc is secured and maintained through the exercise of intellectual and moral leadership in the institutions of civil society. But in a crisis situation, when its leadership has been seriously challenged or weakened, a ruling bloc will typically attempt to retain its dominant position through the exercise of its coercive powers. Its control of the repressive apparatuses of the police and the military often enable it to subordinate other classes even when its hegemony over them is weakened or undermined.

Naturally, within any given social order, the relationship between persuasion and coercion, discourse and force will vary historically (Buci-Glucksmann 1982: 120–121). With this variability in mind, as Frederick Bird has argued, one of the best ways to assess the strength and dynamic character of any particular religious and moral system in a specific time and place is to analyze the extent to which people seek to communicate their expectations and claims to others by non-moral means. Foremost among these non-moral means are the exercise of direct or indirect coercion through the threat or use of police and military force, economic sanctions, personal violence, pillage of property, and the institutionalization of servitude (Bird 1981: 162).

When the social and personal agreements upon which morality rest are strongly and widely shared, resort to coercion and force will be rare. But in historical and social situations when such assumptions and agreements have come to be doubted or openly challenged, the potential for coercive and violent means of regulating human behavior is increased. The power and pervasiveness of these coercive and violent means for controlling and influencing human behavior are obvious. It is also obvious that particular moral systems themselves sometimes seek to justify expressions of coercion and violence. Coercion is often accepted as a legitimate means for controlling and influencing behavior of aliens, criminals, children, and others who may be viewed by a particular community as incapable of acting as morally responsible adults (Bird 1981: 162). One of the main aims of a critical–contextual approach to the study of religion and ethics is "to foster a greater understanding of the functions and dynamic of moral systems by analyzing the interaction and relative saliency of moralities as languages of persuasion and these other non-moral means of exerting social influence" (Bird 1981: 162–163).

As we have seen, Gramsci viewed liberal–democratic political regimes of modern Western societies as systems of hegemonic equilibrium in which force and consent were combined and balanced in varying proportions, without force prevailing too greatly over consent (Fontana 2002: 29). Nonetheless, the ruling ideas of an age must constantly be reasserted and defended—ever new ways must be found to ensure that they hold on to their status as ruling ideas. Thus the medieval Church continuously monitored the outbreak of heretical ways of thinking and reasserted the orthodoxies of Christian dogma. Likewise with the rise of the bourgeoisie in the age of modernity, its ideas, beliefs, and feelings regarding the value of the nation-state, nationalism and patriotism, the value of competition, the inviolability of private property and the individual person, the foundational role of the nuclear family in social organization and reproduction, the generation of self-esteem by selling one's labor-power in work, and the right to render most anything for sale were not so much givens as items of struggle that needed to be reasserted time and again (Boer 2009: 269).

The ongoing struggle to win consent through intellectual and moral persuasion always and only takes place within the broader social–political context of conflict over which attitudes, values, and beliefs will dominate the thought and behavior of people in society. The *need* to persuade people to accept particular views, values, and styles of life only *arises* in the context of a *competition* or *conflict* between alternative views, values, and styles of life. The question I wish to pose at this point is whether Gramsci's ideas can help shed light on the clash of worldviews and values that is taking place in our own time.

Globalization and the New World Order

There is considerable debate among scholars as to whether Gramsci's ideas can be legitimately extended beyond his own national and historical contexts to an analysis of developments in an early twenty-first-century world that he could never have envisioned.[4] As is obvious from the discussion up to this point, I am among those who believe that the relevance of Gramsci's key ideas is not limited to Italy in the first half of the twentieth century. In my effort to relate Gramsci to the study of religion and ethics I concur with political scientist Stephen Gill, who argues for a "symptomatic" reading of Gramsci, a reading that is "productive and developmental" rather than a simple "application" of his ideas to circumstances that are very different from his own, a reading geared toward "translation" (in its broadest sense) of his ideas into terms that make sense of our own situation (2008: xx–xxi).

In his classic account of Gramsci's life and thought, James Joll observed that Gramsci's prison writings were more concerned with analyzing the past and searching for historical lessons than they were with prescribing specific courses of action in the present or planning the details of a new society, which in his life's circumstances must have seemed very remote (1977: 135). One such lesson was that any major historical change, any emergence of a new ruling bloc, was marked by an intellectual and moral reform, by a change in people's consciousness (1977: 138). There is no doubt that Gramsci was primarily concerned with Italy, and it was primarily from the Italian past that he drew examples to illustrate his key ideas. Nonetheless, he demonstrated considerable knowledge of French history and politics, along with many insights into English and American culture. Indeed, in the section of his *Prison Notebooks* titled "Americanism and Fordism," he made many shrewd observations regarding how the absence of a traditional hierarchy of social classes in the United States, as contrasted with Europe, made possible the emergence of "a new human type" in conformity with the new methods for organizing factory labor pioneered by Henry Ford and engineer Frederick W. Taylor, and Gramsci speculated about the prospects that Americanism—"a certain way of life, of thought, of experiencing life"—would eventually spread to Europe and beyond (Gramsci cited in Joll 1977: 136–138; see Gramsci 1971: 277–318).

Besides his broad acquaintance with the history of Western Europe and America, Joll points out that Gramsci's experience with the Comintern meant that he was always aware of international influences and comparisons, and he believed that hegemony could be exercised on an international scale as well as within a single country (139).[5] As Gramsci himself wrote,

> Every relationship of "hegemony" is necessarily an educational relationship and occurs not only within a nation, between the various forces of which the nation is composed, but in the international and world-wide field, between complexes of national and continental civilisations.
>
> (1971: 350)

Gramsci died in 1937, before the structures of world order were remade by the Second World War, the Cold War, and the collapse of international communism. Even so, a number of scholars have argued that his ideas remain relevant for understanding international developments in the latter half of the twentieth and into the first decades of the twenty-first centuries. On this view, Gramsci's ideas can be developed to make sense of a new structure of international power and a new world system in which a particular economic order and a corresponding way of organizing social life have become hegemonic on an international level (Schwarzmantel 2009a: 6).

A "world order" may be understood as a particular configuration of power and authority, rulers and ruled, leaders and led in a given historical epoch (Gill 2008: 47). World politics, international relations, problems of war and peace, and social development all take place within such configurations. Modern history and the development of capitalism have been characterized by several phases of world order. These include: the period of Dutch hegemony and the birth of the so-called "Westphalia system" in 1648 in the aftermath of the Thirty Years' War, which institutionalized the concept of sovereign nation-states; the period of British hegemony and free-trade imperialism; and the period of American hegemony, during which time there has been an increasing globalization of capitalism (Arrighi 1993). In each case, both domestic and international politics must be understood as taking place within a particular global structure in which one model of society is hegemonic, a model of society predominantly exemplified by a particular state and its dominant class (Schwarzmantel 2009a: 6–7). Among the most salient features of these models are their notions of leadership or governance and their conceptions of the proper relationship between political and civil society and the economy.

The period after the Second World War saw the emergence of an international historical bloc under U.S. leadership that represented itself as defending and promoting the security and civilization of the "Free World" against the challenge of Soviet communism. Initially consisting of transatlantic relations between the U.S. and Western Europe, this bloc eventually expanded to include trilateral relations with Japan. As Stephen Gill explains, Gramsci's concept of a "historical bloc" refers to an alliance of different class forces politically organized around a set of hegemonic ideas and values that gives strategic direction and coherence to its constituent elements.

> For a new historic bloc to emerge, its leaders must engage in "conscious, planned struggle" in both political and civil society. Any new historic bloc must have not only power within the civil society and economy but it also needs persuasive ideas, arguments and initiatives that build on, catalyze and develop its political networks and organization.
>
> (Gill 2008: 60–61)

The alliance of core capitalist states that emerged after the Second World War was grounded in a "negotiated consensus among the major industrial interests, organised labour and government" (Robert Cox cited in Schwarzmantel 2009a: 7). This consensus did not come without considerable struggle to establish a measure of social control over capital, but once achieved it provided the basis for what has been described as a system of "embedded liberalism," the model for which was the "internationalisation of the New Deal" (Gill 2008: 60; Robinson 2014: 218).[6] In post-war Europe this took the form of rebuilding or creating liberal democracy and encouraging the political center, class compromise, and "corporatism"—a spirit of collaboration among major interest groups for the sake of the society as a whole. During the period of post-war reconstruction supervised by the American occupation and partially funded by the Marshall Plan, comprehensive efforts were made to introduce more advanced and efficient forms of mass production organized according to principles of "scientific management." At the macroeconomic level, government spending and tax policies followed Keynesian principles to regulate the expansion, to manage growing demand and rising wages, and to fuel mass consumption (Gill 2008: 60).

> The new post-war capitalist political settlements were relatively inclusive and therefore socially hegemonic; they therefore involved moderate organized labour as well as corporate capital, plus leaders from civil society, for example in the media, in the universities, in centrist political parties and from churches. The international framework was both European and transatlantic, and whilst it remained under U.S. leadership the interests of allies and subordinate classes were given weight in decision-making. The bloc thus combined coercion and consent. Fordist accumulation provided the material basis of the system and its material legitimation was through growth in mass consumption. Its ideological and political banners included the concepts of liberty, modernity, affluence, welfare and the "end of ideology". These elements were fused into a concept of 'the West' and an anti-Communist alliance. The historical bloc therefore balanced national and transnational capital, organized labour and the state. It was anchored in the structures of production and social reproduction and in the transnational political and civil societies of the capitalist core (Western Europe and North America).
> (Gill 2008: 61)

However, the post-war liberal consensus between industry, labor, and government began to break down during the 1970s, 1980s, and 1990s as capitalist countries struggled to cope with cycles of inflation and recession, a series of financial crises around the world, and the disruption of domestic industries associated with the increasing globalization of financial and labor markets and shifts in patterns of production and consumption. Multinational corporations, their political allies, and many within the economics profession began to rethink the role of governments, and especially the role of organized labor, in the management and regulation of an increasingly globalized economy. The push to deregulate the economy, cut taxes, privatize formerly public services, and severely curtail the power of labor unions during the Thatcher–Reagan years signaled a transition from "embedded" to "neo"-liberalism within key capitalist states.[7]

Meanwhile, against the background of mounting military and economic pressures on both East and West associated with the arms race, the East Bloc countries were undergoing their own economic crises accompanied by popular and intellectual forces of "civil society" that eventually propelled the overthrow of communism. Yet from a Gramscian perspective, these developments amounted to a "passive revolution" insofar as these popular forces were largely prevented from gaining state power. The newly constituted states that emerged from the process were largely reformed from the top down and incorporated into the capitalist world order through a system of "disciplinary neo-liberalism"—a system that promotes the world market itself as the principal form of governance (Gill 2008: 63).

Reform programs in the former Eastern bloc were carried out under the guidance of external forces from Western Europe and other institutions of global capitalism. The European Union and its G7 allies promoted constitutional reforms that combined protection of liberal freedoms and limited democratization through electoral politics with economic "shock therapy"—rapid privatization and marketization—in an effort to legitimate and accelerate an irreversible transition to capitalism. The new constitutions served to lock in new property rights for capital, placed constraints on political alternatives to neoliberal policies, and thereby helped to eradicate communism and socialism by juridical means. Moreover, the West imposed strict political and economic conditions on the former Eastern bloc nations in exchange for loans, technical assistance, and the right to apply for entry into such organizations as the European Union, NATO, and the World Trade Organization. Similar to the era of the Marshall Plan, the post-communist reforms had the effect of domesticating more radical democratic and populist impulses and rebuilding capitalism. This extended the geographical and political reach of neoliberal social forces by empowering a new bourgeoisie in the East and subordinating or appropriating East European military assets under NATO command. This same logic of disciplinary neoliberalism has been extended throughout many parts of the former "Third World" as well (Gill 2008: 63–64).

Thus, as capitalism has moved beyond a nation-state-centered system to a transnational one, a transnational capitalist "class" or "establishment" has emerged consisting of segments of national bourgeoisies and state bureaucracies from a range of countries "who have material interests in the relatively free flow of capital, goods and services within the world economy" (Gill 2008: 93). This class comprises the core of a transnational historical bloc, key members of which include major owners and managers of transnational corporations, international bankers, and many though not all leading politicians and civil servants in advanced capitalist countries and in some developing countries as well. The growth of this class has been facilitated by innovations in transportation and communication and through the promotion of dialogue and interaction between elites by both private and public institutions (Gill 2008: 93–94).

This transition from an international historical bloc grounded in the nation-state to a more genuinely transnational bloc grounded in global markets has been accompanied by a transition in the role of the state. In the post-Second World War period, liberal welfare states maintained the consent of their populations and sustained their hegemony through both material and ideological means—through the provision of material prosperity and social welfare and through convincing people that the crusade to defend freedom and democracy against the threat of communism united them in a common moral project that transcended their disparate social and class backgrounds.

By contrast, in the post-Cold War period, neoliberal states are more oriented toward the integration of their economies into the global system of production and exchange. This does not necessarily mean that the significance of national states in an increasingly globalized capitalist economy is diminished so much as it means that there has been a transition in which some state functions are curtailed (e.g. social welfare) and others are strengthened (e.g. the facilitation of markets through negotiation of trade agreements, ongoing repression through surveillance and incarceration, and the development of more comprehensive means of monitoring and maintaining "national security" at home and abroad) (Egan 2008: 254).

Ideologies of Globalization

In their efforts to justify and promote the new world order, proponents have deployed what global studies scholar Manfred Steger has called an ideology of "market globalism." For the last several decades, corporate executives, managers, and lobbyists, prominent journalists and academics, political leaders and high-level state bureaucrats, magazines, journals, newspapers, and electronic media have saturated public discourse with idealized images of a consumer lifestyle in a free-market world (Steger 2009b: 102–103). From this perspective, globalization is primarily about the liberalization and integration of markets. Public support for the neoliberal agenda is sought by touting the idea that globalization serves the general interest—it benefits everyone by raising living standards, reducing global poverty, improving economic efficiency, promoting unprecedented technological progress, enhancing individual freedom, and extending democracy around the world (Steger 2009a: 12–13). Moreover, globalization is presented as an inevitable, irreversible, and impersonal process. No one is in charge; it is the result of historical developments and economic laws that are beyond anyone's control (Steger 2009a: 60–87, 2009b: 101–113).

The ideology of market globalism reached its peak during the "Roaring Nineties," an apt phrase coined by Nobel Prize-winning economist Joseph Stiglitz, a former adviser to President Bill Clinton and former chief economist of the World Bank (Steger 2009a: 13, 54–55). However, market globalism has not gone unchallenged. The decades of the late twentieth and early twenty-first centuries have seen ongoing debate about the proper relationship between business, labor, and government; about the role of the state in the provision of social welfare, the regulation of markets, and protection of the natural environment; and about the relationship between consent and coercion—"soft" and "hard" power—in maintaining the stability and security of national and transnational economic and political systems. According to Steger, the three major challengers to market globalism's views on these issues are "national populism," "justice globalism," and "jihadist globalism."

National populism is a genuinely "anti-globalization" stance that has found expression in electoral politics throughout Western Europe, the United States, Australia, New Zealand, and beyond. Even in this era of intensifying global interaction and interdependence on economic, political, cultural, and ecological levels, national populism continues to conceive of "community" in national rather than global terms. National populist leaders like Patrick Buchanan in the U.S., Jean-Marie and Marine Le Pen in France, and Pauline Hanson in Australia advocate economic protectionism as a way of defending jobs, national industries, and traditional ways of life that are disrupted by the free market. They blame immigration and multiculturalism for eroding a sense of national identity and a spirit of patriotism (Steger 2009a: 131–145).

"Justice" and "jihadist" globalisms share national populism's opposition to the neoliberal world order, but it would be inaccurate to describe them as anti-globalization ideologies. Rather, they are better understood as "alter-globalization" perspectives. Justice and jihadist globalisms conceive of the present era in global rather than narrowly national terms, but their visions of a new world order provide alternatives to the one set forth by market globalism (Steger 2009b: 99).

"Justice" or "ethical" globalism envisions a world order based on egalitarian ideals of global solidarity and distributive justice (Steger 2009b: 99; Gill 2009: 104). It contests market globalism's claims regarding the unambiguously positive consequences of neoliberal policies, arguing instead that the liberalization and integration of markets has led to growing disparities between rich and poor, a weakening of participatory forms of democracy and a marginalization of the powerless, an escalation of global conflicts and violence, the proliferation of greed and consumerism, and environmental destruction on a catastrophic scale. It also contests the inevitability of market globalism's version of globalization. Rejecting Margaret Thatcher's famous claim that 'there is no alternative' to a neoliberal world order, the global justice movement insists that 'another world is possible' (Steger 2009a: 128–129).

The global justice movement consists of countless networks of citizens, activists, scholars, and non-governmental organizations that together constitute what they view as a "global civil society."[8] Participants are linked through social media, the internet, and other means of global communication, and they meet in various venues and forums around the world, one of the largest of which is the World Social Forum (WSF). The WSF defines itself as

> an open meeting place for reflective thinking, democratic debate of ideas, formulation of proposals, free exchange of experiences and inter-linking for effective action, by groups and movements of civil society

that are opposed to neo-liberalism and to domination of the world by capital and any form of imperialism, and are committed to building a society centred on the human person.

(World Social Forum 2006)

With annual meetings held at sites throughout the world, the WSF was deliberately created in 2001 as a counterpart to the World Economic Forum (WEF) in Davos, Switzerland. Justice globalists disseminate their ideological and policy alternatives via the WSF just as the WEF is used as a platform for projecting the ideas and values of market globalism (Steger 2009b: 115).

Among the alternatives proposed by various global justice advocates is the implementation of a "global New Deal"—a worldwide program of taxation and redistribution similar to what was introduced at the national level in Western countries a century ago—and a "global Marshall Plan" that would include forgiveness of Third World debt. More specifically, there is widespread support among justice globalists for levying the so-called "Tobin Tax" (named after Nobel Prize-winning economist James Tobin) on international short-term financial transactions. Such a measure would arguably discourage risky currency speculation and stabilize exchange rates while supporting human development initiatives in poor countries via the revenue collected from the tax. Other proposals include the abolition of offshore financial centers offering tax havens for wealthy individuals and corporations, implementation of stringent environmental agreements, establishment of international labor protection standards (perhaps as clauses included in a profoundly reformed WTO), greater transparency and accountability to citizens by national governments and global economic institutions, making all governance of globalization explicitly gender sensitive, and the transformation of "free trade" into "fair trade" (Steger 2009a: 129–130, 2009b: 121).

The global justice "movement" is a very disparate and loose-knit collection of actors, perhaps better described as a "movement of movements." It encompasses both reformist and revolutionary tendencies, and it employs a broad range of tactics. What unity it has comes not from a centralized leadership or common political platform but rather from recognition of common problems, empathy with the suffering of others, and commitment to democratic principles of collective action (Gill 2009: 107). The Zapatista uprising in Chiapas, Mexico, on the very day that the North American Free Trade Agreement (NAFTA) took effect in 1994, is one of the more militant expressions of the global justice movement. Justice globalism has also fueled protests at summit meetings of the WTO, IMF, World Bank, World Economic Forum, and other gatherings of global elites by hundreds of thousands of demonstrators in the streets of Seattle, Davos, Washington, D.C., Chang Mai, Melbourne, Prague, Gothenburg, Genoa, Cancun, and beyond. The Occupy Wall Street Movement in the U.S. and the anti-austerity movements in Spain and Greece that emerged in response to the financial crisis and "Great Recession" of the late 2000s can also be viewed as expressions of justice globalism. Although less attention-getting than uprisings and street protests, ideas and values associated with justice globalism have also been introduced into electoral politics by established Green parties in Europe and by dissident Democrats and Independents like Dennis Kucinich and Bernie Sanders, as well as third-party candidates like Ralph Nader in the U.S., and they have been championed by many religious leaders and organizations, as we will see in more detail below.

"Jihadist globalism" is a label that applies to various ideologies on the religious right—including non-Muslim religious fundamentalisms—that call for establishing a global religious community by means of violent struggle against the forces of secularism and false belief (Steger 2009a: 147–148). The most successful expression of this alternative vision of globalization has been Osama bin Laden's al Qaeda and its various spin-offs, including the "Islamic State" in Iraq and Syria (ISIS). Jihadist globalism opposes both market and justice globalism as it seeks to radicalize and mobilize the worldwide community of Muslims—the *ummah*—to defend the values and beliefs of a particular version of Islam that are thought to have been betrayed by corrupt ruling elites in Muslim countries, threatened by the forces of secularism and consumerism, and attacked by Western military interventions in the Muslim world. The restoration of God's rule on earth is not a local, national, or regional enterprise, but a concerted global effort spearheaded by jihadists operating in various localities around the world (2009b: 99, 124).

After al Qaeda's attacks on 9/11, the ideological struggle of the twenty-first century entered a new phase, with market globalism morphing into what Steger has described as "imperial globalism"—a merger of neoliberalism's promotion of free markets with neoconservatism's emphasis on national security and the projection of American military power. The distinguishing feature of this new "imperial" phase of market globalism is the claim that the ongoing liberalization and integration of markets and the promotion of freedom and democracy around the world will require an ongoing U.S.-led Global War on Terror (Steger 2009a: 87–95).[9]

A Competition of Global Ethics

The religious and ethical dimensions of the ideological struggle over the neoliberal world order were becoming apparent even before the advent of the global war on terror. Buddhist philosopher David Loy argued in 1997 that "market capitalism ... has already become the most successful religion of all time, winning more converts more quickly than any previous belief system or value-system in human history" (1997: 276). Loy explained that the "religion of the market" provides "a worldview, with ontology and ethics, in competition with other understandings of what the world is and how we should live in it" (1997: 278). With the market as its god, the discipline of economics as its theology, and the advertising industry as its missionary vanguard, the religion of market capitalism promises salvation through ever-increasing production and consumption (while simultaneously concealing the spiritual dissatisfaction, social injustice, and environmental destruction that result from this false promise). In a 1999 article in *The Atlantic*, Christian theologian Harvey Cox described the rise of an increasingly influential "business theology" that revolved around the idea of "The Market as God," and he argued that faith in The Market had become one of the main competitors with the world's traditional religious worldviews and ethics (Cox 1999). For his part, economist Robert H. Nelson has written of the "New Holy Wars" that pit "economic religion" and "environmental religion" against one another in a struggle for the soul of contemporary societies (Nelson 2001, 2010).

As for the world's more traditional religions, some of their leaders and adherents appear to have made their peace with the neoliberal world order— they simply ignore the economic, ethical–political, and ecological issues that arise in connection with global capitalism; or they preach a gospel of wealth or personal therapy that conforms to the materialism and individualism of the present world order; or they adapt to a status quo in which religion itself is marketed as one commodity among others that consumers might find appealing enough to incorporate into their personal lifestyle choices. Other religious leaders and communities have aligned themselves with national populism's nostalgia for the past or with the militantly anti-secular agendas of jihadism and other forms of fundamentalism.

Of greater interest for the present project are those religious leaders, adherents, and organizations that have positioned themselves at the forefront of the global justice movement, drawing on their traditions as a resource for justice globalism's moral critique of the neoliberal world order and its vision of a more humane, democratic, peaceful, and ecological future. Pope Francis, the Dalai Lama, the World Council of Churches, and countless other people of faith have openly challenged the greed, materialism, individualism, violence, inequality, and environmental destruction that they believe is being fueled by the global economy.[10]

To be sure, global capitalism has generated wealth on a scale that is unprecedented in human history, along with technological innovations that have unleashed revolutions in transportation and communication. As Muslim political scientist Chandra Muzaffar has noted, this facilitation of human interaction across cultural borders and religious boundaries is an accomplishment of the global economy that religious men and women should applaud, insofar as the ideal of a universal human community lies at the heart of many of the world's religious traditions (Knitter and Muzaffar 2002: 154).

But alongside the global economy's accomplishments are distressing material and moral failures. While poverty has been in decline worldwide, improvements in life spans, education, and incomes have been slowing due to natural disasters, misguided government policies and worsening inequality in a world where the 85 richest people have as much wealth as the 3.5 billion poorest people. More than 2.2 billion people remain "poor or near-poor," with financial crises, natural disasters, soaring food prices, and violent conflicts threatening to exacerbate the problem. About 1.2 billion people survive on the equivalent of $1.25 or less per day (Kurtenbach 2014; UNHDR 2014).

A striking example of a religiously grounded moral critique of the neoliberal world order can be seen in the "Declaration toward a Global Ethic" promulgated by the Parliament of the World's Religions. The declaration argues that in the aftermath of the twentieth century's world wars, the collapse of Fascism and Nazism, the breakdown of communism and colonialism, and the technological, economic, political, and cultural transformations wrought by globalization, "humanity has entered a new phase of history."

> Today we possess sufficient economic, cultural, and spiritual resources to introduce a better global order, but old and new *ethnic, national, social, economic, and religious tensions* threaten the peaceful building of a better world. We have experienced greater technological progress than ever before, yet we see that world-wide poverty, hunger, death of children, unemployment, misery, and the destruction of nature have not diminished but rather have increased. Many peoples are threatened with economic ruin, social disarray, political marginalization, ecological catastrophe, and moral collapse.
>
> (Küng and Kuschel 1995: 19, emphasis in original)

Against this background of "crisis in global economy, global ecology, and global politics," the declaration proclaims that there can be "no new global order without a new global ethic … Without such a fundamental consensus on an ethic, sooner or later every community will be threatened by chaos or dictatorship, and individuals will despair" (Küng and Kuschel 1995: 17–18, 21).

The declaration alleges that "a minimal *fundamental consensus* concerning binding *values, irrevocable standards*, and fundamental *moral attitudes*" already exists in the teachings of the world's religions. While acknowledging that "this ethic provides no direct solution for all the immense problems of the world," it nonetheless does supply the basis for "a *vision* which can lead women and men away from despair, and society away from chaos" (Küng and Kuschel 1995: 18, emphasis in original). This vision begins with the fundamental demand that "every human being must be treated humanely," a demand long recognized by the world's great religious and ethical traditions in the form of the "golden rule" (Küng and Kuschel 1995: 21, 23). The declaration goes on to identify "four irrevocable directives" that are "implied" by this fundamental principle:

1   Commitment to a culture of non-violence and respect for life.
2   Commitment to a culture of solidarity and a just economic order.
3   Commitment to a culture of tolerance and a life of truthfulness.
4   Commitment to a culture of equal rights and partnership between men and women.

(Küng and Kuschel 1995: 24–34)

These four directives seek to articulate an alternative to the dominant moral languages of our time: a language of *wisdom* to counterbalance *scientism* and to warn against the misuse of scientific research; a language of *spirituality* to counterbalance the *discourse of technology* and to help keep the risks of efficient but morally ambiguous technologies under control; a language of *ecology* to counterbalance the *discourse of industry* and to help place limits on an ever-expanding economy and consumer lifestyle; and a language of *justice* to complement a *discourse of freedom and democracy* that sometimes masks the concentration of power and wealth in the hands of fewer and fewer people (Küng and Kuschel 1995: 98).[11]

Framing the discussion of world order in terms of ethics has been a hallmark of both the religious and secular participants in the movement for global peace and justice. Issues of economics and politics are always set within the context of an overarching moral question: what is the present world order doing to and for people and the natural environment?

While some powerful leaders and institutions continue to advocate "business as usual," there is increasing recognition that this is precisely what has led to the financial crises, inequalities, social upheavals, failed states, prolonged military conflicts, and ecological catastrophes that have characterized life in the early twenty-first century. Even many advocates of market globalism have conceded that globalization has been "mismanaged" and that reforms are necessary. In an effort to put a more "human face" on global capitalism, there have been increasing calls for greater "corporate responsibility" and more "inclusive globalization." In search of greater consent and legitimacy, some of the more farsighted sectors of the global business community have borrowed the notion of "sustainability" from the discourse of justice globalism and now profess their commitment to the "triple bottom line"—"people" and "planet" as well as "profits." Others have shifted from market-based shareholder capitalism toward stakeholder models more attuned to the needs of communities. Increasing numbers of companies tout their leadership role in addressing corruption, water shortages, infectious diseases, disaster relief, pollution, and climate change (Gill 2009: 103–102; Steger 2009a: 160–161).

The importance of these moderate reforms should not be minimized. While the rhetoric surrounding sustainable development and other "responsible" business practices may sometimes amount to little more than "greenwashing," a public relations strategy that simply seeks to mask business as usual, many of these reforms have had significant impacts on the lives of local and regional communities (Bird et al. 2016). However, beyond the question of the sincerity and authenticity of these top-down reforms to the existing system, the question remains as to whether they will be enough to adequately address the range of problems that must be faced.

As mentioned above, there are many within the global justice movement who have called for a far more extensive reform agenda. A "global New Deal" would subject the global marketplace to greater democratic accountability by means of more effective regulatory institutions. The philosophies and structures of existing institutions—the IMF, World Bank, and WTO among them—would be dramatically revamped or dismantled; the new institutions and policies would prioritize the needs of people and the environment over the imperatives of capital. The impetus for such change comes from deteriorating social and environmental conditions that have galvanized global networks of industrial and urban workers, peasants, farmers, indigenous peoples, experts in science and technology, ecologists, feminists, socialists, peace activists, and people of faith seeking to pressure market globalists to come to the negotiating table before the world descends into devastation beyond repair. It is argued that only something like a global New Deal will be able to reverse the steady rise of inequality and environmental degradation, preserve some version of a global economy, and prevent the growth of national populism and jihadism with their anti- and alt-globalization agendas (Steger 2009a: 130, 162, 166; Brown 2009).

A more radical wing of the global justice movement insists that even these reforms will not be enough and that more far-reaching changes are needed. While a global New Deal would help to alleviate inequality and other social problems associated with neoliberal globalization, it would not resolve the systemic nature of these problems nor would it adequately address the ecological crisis facing the planet. This wing of the movement has called not for the reform of global capitalism, but for the creation of a new post-capitalist order.

Reform and/or Revolution?

At the core of capitalism is the imperative for the system to constantly expand. A reformed no less than a neoliberal version of global capitalism must seek continued economic growth. Yet the ever expanding economic system is placing increasing burdens on a fixed earth system to the point of planetary overload (Robinson 2014: 229; Boggs 2012; Rees 2011, 2014; Brown 2009). To be sure, previous civilizations (Sumerians, Mayans, and others) have overshot the ability of their local ecosystems to sustain them and have collapsed as a result. What makes the current situation unique is the scale and pace at which the global economy is outstripping the capacity of natural systems to renew themselves.

> The current moment is distinct in that this time the collapse would be that of global civilization. We face the prospect of a more far-reaching systemic implosion in the twenty-first century through ecological crisis—as suggested in global climate change; peak oil and other resource depletion scenarios; the spiral of species extinctions; and scientific predictions of a collapse of central agricultural systems in China, Australia, the U.S. Midwest, and other global breadbaskets in the coming decades.
>
> (Robinson 2014: 230)[12]

Of course the ecological and social dimensions of the crises facing the neoliberal world order are connected. Extreme weather events, desertification, ocean acidification, melting glaciers, mass extinctions, and rising sea levels are projected to bring about widespread famine, proliferating disease, millions of climate refugees, and increased political instability over the next few decades (Robinson 2014: 231–232). It is against this backdrop that the Pentagon has begun preparing for what Michael Parenti has described as the "militarized management of civilization's violent disintegration" (quoted in Robinson 2014: 232).[13] This is also the backdrop against which the radical wing of the global justice movement insists on the need to replace global capitalism with a post-capitalist world order in which humanity is no longer at war with itself and with nature (Robinson 2014: 232).

Here we can see that the global justice movement has run up against the same classic question that confronted the socialist movement during Gramsci's time—reform or revolution? Reformists, then and now, argue that present problems are so urgent that they must be addressed immediately (even if only partially) through pragmatic strategies of mitigation and adaptation that work within the existing system. Revolutionaries ask whether it is more utopian to believe that the crisis can be resolved within the confines of the system than to believe that the system can and must be overthrown (Robinson 2014: 229).

As William I. Robinson argues (2014), it would seem that reforming and superseding the system of global capitalism are both necessary and must be mutually reinforcing. People's local struggles to address the problems that disrupt and undermine the conditions of their day-to-day existence are almost by definition reformist struggles. Yet from a Gramscian perspective, what is required is that leaders within the global justice movement move beyond reformism by articulating and winning support for an alternative vision that moves from challenging the "fairness" of the market to replacing the logic of the market with a social and ecological logic (Robinson 2014: 233).

Any number of thinkers and organizations have been working to articulate the elements of such an alternative vision.[14] Among the most significant of these elements is a fundamental shift in the way we think about economic development and human progress. Calculations of economic development routinely rely on such purely quantitative measures as Gross Domestic Product (GDP), yet the GDP is merely a sum of national spending with no distinctions between transactions that add to human and environmental wellbeing and those that diminish it (Redefining Progress n.d.). For example, the GDP often counts pollution as a double gain: once when it is created, and then again when it is cleaned up. While a problem like pollution clearly detracts from the quality of life, the industrial activity that caused it in the first place and the money spent to clean it up both contribute to economic "growth" as calculated by the GDP. When standard economic indicators focus simply on the sheer amount of economic activity without making any qualitative distinctions between kinds of activity, they present a fraudulent picture of reality. The GDP conceals vast levels of waste and destruction of resources; it bears little relationship to the general quality of life of most people as measured by levels of education and housing, health and medical care, democratic access, working conditions, quality of infrastructure, and natural resource supports (Boggs 2012: 169).

Alternative ways of measuring economic outcomes and societal wealth— such as the Genuine Progress Indicator (GPI), the Green GDP, the Index of Sustainable Economic Welfare, or the Gross National Happiness measure (Rampell 2008)—provide a basis for rethinking and fundamentally transforming structures and practices throughout the economy including banking, healthcare, energy and transportation, agriculture, military spending, and executive pay. According to Carl Boggs and other researchers, reductions in deep and systemic waste and destruction in the present economy, along with a protracted shift toward more equitable, efficient, and sustainable modes of production, consumption, and distribution, could reduce "growth" and permit significant cuts in the GDP while supporting *increased* living standards for the general population. (Boggs 2012: 171, 174; Rees 2011, 2014).

An equitable and sustainable steady-state economy is not to be confused with a static economy. While the economy must not continue to "grow" at the expense of people and the earth's capacity to support those people, it can continue to develop. Indeed, new firms and even whole industrial sectors can develop and even expand as their equivalents in obsolete or "sunset" industries are phased out (Rees 2011: 14).

A Post-Modern Prince? Hegemony and Counter-Hegemony in the Global Age

From a Gramscian perspective, the explicit challenges posed to market globalism by various ideological alternatives, along with neoliberalism's increasing reliance on coercive rather than persuasive means of maintaining world order, suggests a "crisis of authority" that opens up the possibility for critique and struggle by subordinate groups whose interests are not being addressed by the dominant system (Howson 2011: 169). While global elites may have reached consensus about rolling back the redistributive policies of the mid-twentieth-century welfare and social–democratic states, vast numbers of people around the world have failed to internalize and consent to the neoliberal agenda. Whatever degree of hegemony neoliberalism has been able to achieve, it is far weaker than the more expansive hegemony achieved during the era of embedded liberalism, with its combination of ideological leadership and material rewards. The more restricted hegemony of neoliberalism may be said to rest less on the consent than on the disorganization of popular classes and their systematic disempowerment by neoliberal policies (Robinson 2014: 217).

Granting the fact that early twenty-first-century circumstances are very different from those in the first half of the twentieth, a question that arises in our own time is very similar to one that Gramsci faced, namely, how might it be possible to bring about a transformation of consciousness—an "intellectual and moral reformation"—that would set the stage for the establishment of a new world order (in this case a post-neoliberal world order), and who or what might be the agent of such a change?

As we saw in chapter three, Gramsci shared the standard Marxist belief that the organized working class—the proletariat—would be the necessary agent of revolutionary social change in modern industrialized societies. In his early writings he viewed factory councils as institutions capable of creating and diffusing a new mentality and ethic that would challenge the established society. Later, in the *Prison Notebooks*, Gramsci shifted his attention to the political party—the "Modern Prince"—as the chief agent of radical change. A revolutionary political party would play the leading role in educating and mobilizing the working class and thereby provide the vehicle for a wholesale intellectual and moral transformation of society (Schwarzmantel 2009b: 81–85).

Needless to say, neither of these models of political agency seems very plausible in the contemporary context. Changes in the nature and organization of production have displaced large factories with a fixed workforce; accompanying changes in social structure have left the classical proletariat a minority presence in the wider society (Schwarzmantel 2009b: 85–87). Organized labor remains a significant force in some sectors of the economy, and some labor unions have played a leading role in the global justice movement. However, the working class as a whole has not been a cohesive nor a particularly progressive political force in the late twentieth and early twenty-first centuries. It has often failed to transcend its own narrow economic interests (for example, when it comes to issues such as jobs versus environmental protection), and it has not been possible to count on the proletariat to support, much less to lead, a fundamental transformation of society.

The likelihood that factory councils could play the transformative role that Gramsci once envisaged for them was small enough in his own time; it appears even less likely in ours. Meanwhile, the role of political parties in contemporary politics is a far cry from what Gramsci had in mind. As we have seen, Gramsci believed that a mass political party, properly organized and led, could raise peoples' consciousness above a purely economic level and diffuse a new worldview and corresponding norm of life; it would spread the myth of a new order in the Sorelian sense, inspiring people to action. Today it is difficult to imagine political parties fulfilling Gramsci's scenario of a modern Prince (Schwarzmantel 2009b: 87–88).

Political parties in contemporary liberal–democratic societies do not typically function as incubators of new worldviews and ethics nor as agents of fundamental social and economic transformation. Rather, they assume the status quo in much the same way that rival athletic teams assume the rules of the game; they act as organizations for rallying support behind particular leaders and getting out the vote during regular rituals of electoral competition. Politics itself is presented as a matter of individual choice rather than collective purpose, with consumers picking which party's "brand" best satisfies them. The political party's role becomes one of marketing, accentuating the differences (often very superficial ones) with opposing parties, and responding via focus groups to people's preferences as they are, rather than engaging in the serious critical and educational work that Gramsci called for (Schwarzmantel 2009b: 88).

Yet while the Marxist myth of the proletariat is not tenable, and while political parties as presently conceived seem unlikely vehicles for a fundamental transformation of consciousness, there are still reasons for believing that a Gramscian perspective poses the general problem of political agency in a way that remains relevant to contemporary circumstances (Schwarzmantel 2009b: 79). Stephen Gill, for example, has applied this perspective to the global justice movement, arguing that it might well represent the emergence of a new form of political agency—something like a transnational political party—that could play the role of a "postmodern Prince" in contemporary society.

> [O]ur basic hypothesis is that there is a new fluid form of a transnational political party in formation. It is not institutionalized nor under centralized control. It should be understood as something plural. The new "party" is both a movement and a process, one that is social, economic, ecological and political. It simultaneously involves an ethical and pedagogical moment that is associated with feasible utopias. It has a novel, multiple, flexible and capillary form. In sum this *postmodern Prince* embodies a moment of hope to progressive forces; indeed it is central to the way that they not only imagine but also make another world possible.
> (Gill 2009: 109 emphasis in original)

As we have seen, the global justice movement makes a virtue of the fact that it is not a political party in a traditional sense. It consists of very disparate actors and is only very loosely organized, and the capture of state power has typically not figured as a prominent part of its agenda. Nonetheless, the case for seeing the global justice movement in Gramscian terms rests on the idea that its purpose is to transform mass consciousness, to challenge the hegemony of neoliberalism, and to promote the idea that another world is possible. The parallel between a "modern" and "postmodern" Prince presumably lies in their role of challenging the grip of existing ideas and bringing about an intellectual and moral reformation of the social order (Schwarzmantel 2009b: 88–89; McNally 2009).

Yet the viability and potential of the global justice movement to bring about genuine change will depend on its ability to overcome significant political and practical problems. Among the most significant of these are the movement's approach to leadership and organization, its overly abstract and cosmopolitan ideology, and a political strategy that fails to adequately address the power of the nation-state (McNally 2009; Robinson 2014: 214–238).

Within the ranks of the global justice movement there has been considerable antagonism toward the instrumentalism and careerism often associated with "traditional politics." A hallmark of the movement is its determination to resist centralized leadership and to maintain a transparent and fully democratic structure. Not only does this distinguish it from its neoliberal opponents (the WTO, IMF, and World Bank), it is also a way to foreshadow the emergence of a new more democratic world order. An emphasis on participatory rather than representative democracy militates against the emergence of a professional centralized leadership. The consensus method employed by the movement's various "social forums" typically involves laborious and multi-level consultation in order to maximize participation and protect the "unitary–plural" nature of the movement (McNally 2009: 68).

However laudable the goals of maximum and equal participation, transparency, and consensus might be, from a Gramscian perspective they should not be pursued to such a degree that they end up undermining the effectiveness and popularity of the movement. As we saw in the preceding chapter, Gramsci argued that building an effective movement for social transformation would not only require widespread consultation and consent between "leaders and led" and the avoidance of a bureaucratized leadership, but also a measure of more centralized and directive leadership ("Jacobinism") able to drive forward the movement's program. Critics argue that such leadership has been missing from the global justice movement, where variants of anarchism have figured prominently among some segments of the movement, especially among youth. A tendency to become bogged down in endless consultation and negotiation on the one hand, or a glorification of spontaneous revolt and suspicion of political theory and organization on the other hand, have undermined both the effectiveness and popularity of the global justice movement (McNally 2009: 68–69; Robinson 2014: 221–223).

A second problem is the overly abstract and cosmopolitan quality of the ideology of justice globalism. Recalling Gramsci's emphasis on the importance of linking struggles for social change with national–popular traditions, it might be argued that the movement's critique of neoliberalism and advocacy of global justice often lack the cultural specificity that is capable of mobilizing people with reference to their own particular circumstances (McNally 2009: 69). To the extent that a rhetoric of global citizenship, human rights, health, environmental protection, and sustainability remains abstract and fails to resonate at local and national levels, it risks becoming the preserve of activist elites whose militant globalism appears irrelevant to the masses of people who remain embedded in national and local ideological contexts. Indeed, from a Gramscian perspective, the cause of global justice is unlikely to be furthered until its advocates have developed a strategy and language that is able to persuade people why their own local variant of neoliberalism should be resisted and replaced by a form of social–economic and political order that will address their specific concerns and needs (McNally 2009: 70–71).

A third problem is that the global justice movement has employed a political strategy that fails to confront the power of the state. With the notable exception of Green parties in various countries around the world, many within the movement seem to assume that politics is best carried out "in the streets" or by means of "awareness campaigns" or by creating "local spaces" supposedly detachable from the system of global capitalism rather than by political struggles within the institutions of nation-states.[15] Its most distinctive tactics are its counter summits, protests, and campaigns that focus on the transnational institutions of neoliberalism (McNally 2009: 71–72; Robinson 2014: 232–238). The inadequacy of this strategy is illustrated by the fact that many of the goals sought by justice globalism—protection and reinforcement of the welfare state, extension of union rights, agrarian reform, taxation of financial transactions, multilateral agreements promoting peace and protecting the environment—can only be implemented by national governments (McNally 2009: 72). Moreover, such organizations as the European Union and United Nations, which some global justice theorists and activists hope might carry out the "politicization" and "socialization" of the world economic order, are themselves constrained by and answerable to national governments and their electorates. Decisions made by transnational political organizations are inherently unstable and unlikely to carry weight unless they enjoy solid support in the democratic institutions and among the masses of a significant majority of the nation-states that they remain ultimately accountable to. As Mark McNally argues, calls for organizations like the EU and UN to play a leading role in transforming the world economy "will need to be preceded by a genuine process that occurs from below."

> *Below* in this sense—and in contrast to the [the global justice movement's] exclusive emphasis on civil society—refers primarily to the need for political parties or coalitions to be in power across a broad range of major states that have managed to win widespread support for a programme that articulates popular demands at the national level to the wider goals of an alternative globalisation.
>
> (McNally 2009: 72)

McNally and other critics are right to argue that unless and until the ideology and approach of the global justice movement has been rebalanced so as to more effectively articulate national–popular with global frames of reference, it is unlikely that it can play the role of a "post-modern Prince" in bringing about a genuine transformation of world order.

Conclusion

As the twenty-first century unfolds, a range of post-modern "religions" and "global ethics" are vying for hegemony in the era of globalization: the "religion of the market" with its corresponding ethic of economic growth and consumerism, the "religion of nationalism and militarism" with its corresponding ethic of national security, as well as various religious and secular "fundamentalisms" that have sprung up throughout the world with their ethics of exclusivism and their endless proselytizing on behalf of tradition, science, church, caliphate, progress, party, race, or whatever other gods they have committed themselves to worship. In the meantime, the world's traditional religions have not only *not* disappeared from the contemporary scene—in many cases they appear to be enjoying a resurgence in the global age.

There are many empirical and methodological questions that can be raised about the neo-Gramscian account of world order that I have presented in this chapter. These questions continue to be actively debated, most especially in the fields of international relations and international political economy, and also within the global justice movement itself.[16] Apart from my general contention that a Gramscian framework remains relevant for understanding the question of world order in our contemporary age, I have not sought to defend a specific position in these debates. Rather, I have simply tried to illustrate a useful way of looking at globalization and at the ideological struggle over the shape of world order and disorder in the global age. I have also identified some questions about political agency that must be addressed by any movement seeking to bring about an intellectual and moral transformation of that order. While the odds against such a transformation may appear overwhelming, history reminds us that shifts in world order are inevitable and that radical change frequently occurs when it is least expected (McNally 2009: 74). The question is whether that change will consist in the creation of a more humane and sustainable future or in the collapse of a civilization that destroyed the human and natural systems upon which it depended for its survival.

Notes

1 Within the "romantic" grouping, Lincoln includes such thinkers as those of the êcole sociologique (Emile Durkheim and Marcel Mauss), the functionalist school of social anthropology (Bronislaw Malinowski and A.R. Radcliffe-Brown), and the Chicago school of the history of religions (Mircea Eliade). Within the "materialist" position Lincoln includes Marx (although not necessarily Engels), Max Glucksman and the Manchester school of social anthropology, and the French semiologist Roland Barthes (Lincoln 2003: 77–78).

2 For a more extensive discussion of Gramsci's distinction between "indirect" and "passive" forms of consent on the one hand, and "direct" and "active" consent on the other, see Buci-Glucksmann (1982).

3 Francesco Guicciardini (1483–1540) was an Italian statesman, diplomat, and historian and a contemporary of Machiavelli.

4 For overviews of these debates see Morton 2003; Schwarzmantel 2009a.

5 The Communist International—Comintern for short—was an international association of communist parties founded in 1919 to advocate world revolution. As mentioned briefly in chapter one, Gramsci served in 1922 as the Italian party's delegate to the Comintern in Moscow.

6 Political scientist John Ruggie adapted the term "embedded liberalism" from *The Great Transformation*, Karl Polanyi's classic account of the rise of the modern market economy and the nation-state. Ruggie and others have used it to describe the international economic system among capitalist states from the end of Second World War to the 1970s.

7 "Neoliberalism" refers to the revival of an economic perspective rooted in the "classical" liberal or free-market ideals associated with Adam Smith (1723–1790), David Ricardo (1772–1823), and Herbert Spencer (1820–1903). It advocates individualism, competition, and "free trade" and opposes the regulation of markets and government provision of social welfare (Steger 2009a: 10–13).

8 See Buttigieg (2005) on divergences between many contemporary uses of "civil society" and Gramsci's own use of the concept.

9 There is an extensive literature and ongoing debate about the use of the terms "empire" and "imperial" to describe America's role in the post-Cold War world. For an overview of these debates and a critique of the way in which these terms are often used, see Agnew (2005).

10 See Francis (2015), Dalai Lama (1999), World Council of Churches (2003), Knitter and Muzaffar (2002).

11 See Bird et al. (2016) regarding the leading role played by the global interfaith movement in promoting the practices of global ethics.

12 Lester Brown (2009) makes a parallel argument, but contends that a significantly reformed market-based system can address such problems.

13 See U.S. Department of Defence (2014).

14 See, for example, Boggs (2012); Brown (2009); Daly and Cobb (1994); Rees (2011 and 2014).

15 These are among the tactics explored in Day (2005).

16 For a very useful overview of these debates see McNally and Schwarzmantel (2009).

5 Religion, Ethics, and the Discourses of Social Change

We began the preceding chapter with an overview of functionalist, Marxist, and Gramscian perspectives on religion, ethics, and social order. Yet from the revolt of Anabaptist peasants in sixteenth-century Germany to the Islamic revolution in twentieth-century Iran, from the abolitionist movement of the nineteenth century to the civil rights movement and the New Christian Right in the twentieth, history makes clear that religious and moral ideas do not always function in such a way as to maintain social order and reproduce the status quo. They can also serve as vehicles for criticism and social change. It is therefore necessary to move beyond a preoccupation with "religions of the status quo" in order to account for "religions of resistance," "rebellion," and "revolution" (Lincoln 2003: 77–92). It is necessary to add to the metaphor of religion as "opium" the notion of religion as a "weapon." It is to a consideration of some of the theoretical issues surrounding the relationship between religious ethics and struggles for social change that we now turn.

The Problem of Determinism in Marx, Weber, and Gramsci

One of the main issues that arises in connection with inquiry into religious ethics and social change is the familiar yet complex question about the role and influence of ideas in social and historical development. Here we confront the problem of *determinism* – the question of whether and to what extent religious and moral ideas and discourses are passive *reflections* of underlying material realities, or whether they can play an active and even leading role in shaping and changing such realities.

The main outlines of the standard Marxist approach to this problem are well known. As we saw in chapter one, Marx and Engels wrote in *The German Ideology* that "It is not consciousness that determines life, but life that determines consciousness" (Marx and Engels 1976: 37). Likewise, Marx's Preface to *A Contribution to the Critique of Political Economy* states that "It is not the consciousness of men that determines their being, but, on the contrary, their social being that determines their consciousness" (Marx and Engels 1968: 182).

It is important to recognize that Marx's and Engels' own views of the relationship between social being and consciousness, "structure" and "superstructure", is more complicated than it might appear from these passages, as Engels sought to make clear in his 1890 letter to Joseph Bloch.[1] Nonetheless, these claims about the "determination" of the ideological superstructure by the economic base have often been interpreted in a simplistic and mechanistic fashion by Marxists and non-Marxists alike. From the economic structure of a given society arises an "ideological superstructure"—certain forms of law, a certain kind of state, and certain forms of religious, ethical, political, and aesthetic consciousness, which together function to legitimate the power of those who own the means of economic production. Ideas and discourses are simply "epiphenomena"—the reflection of objective material realities.

As discussed in chapters one and two, a distinguishing feature of Gramsci's work was his rebellion against just this form of determinism, which he rightly believed had come to dominate the mainstream Marxism of his time. Gramsci largely accepted historical materialism's emphasis on the primacy of the mode of production in shaping social and historical development. He believed that economic factors were particularly important for analyzing periods of stability or periods of slow gradual change when the established order of society persisted more or less intact (Boggs 1976: 36).

However, Gramsci insisted that the Marxist analysis of ideology would have to move beyond any simple form of economic determinism if it was to succeed in understanding the complex interplay of diverse forces during what he described as "conjunctural" periods of social transformation—vital periods of upheaval, conflict, and fundamental change in history and society. He thus rejected any notion that there is a mechanical correspondence between structure and superstructure.

> The claim presented as an essential postulate of historical materialism, that every fluctuation of politics and ideology can be presented and expounded as an immediate expression of the structure, must be contested in theory as primitive infantilism, and combated in practice with the authentic testimony of Marx, the author of concrete historical and political works.
>
> (Gramsci 1971: 407)[2]

For Gramsci, ideological expressions such as religion and morality are not merely the passive reflections of the economic base. On the contrary, while religion, philosophy, morality, and art cannot by themselves change the course of history, they can and frequently do play an active role in such change (Eagleton 2007: 112–117). Carl Boggs has summarised Gramsci's rethinking of the base-superstructure metaphor.

> [I]nstead of conceiving of the superstructure as a simple reflection of the economic base, Gramsci viewed the relationship as constantly changing

and reciprocal in its historical complexity; politics, ideas, religion, and culture may not be autonomous in any "ultimate" sense, but their causal power in any given transitional period could be overriding. The dynamic relation of forces at work in any society during a particular time span should be investigated as systematically as possible, rather than assumed in dogmatic fashion, or derived from a set of universally valid propositions.

(Boggs 1976: 36–37)

This reformulation of the base–superstructure metaphor, and this apparent willingness to regard historical materialism as a set of empirical theses rather than as a system of metaphysical truths, has led at least one writer to describe Gramsci as the "Weber of Marxism" (Bocock 1986: 88; see also Shafir 2002). And, in fact, there are a number of striking similarities between Gramsci's approach to religious ethics and social change and that of the great German sociologist.

At the very heart of both Gramsci's and Max Weber's work is an effort to include religious and moral conceptions of the world within a broader theoretical framework that views the economic mode of production as fundamental but not fully determining (Bocock 1986: 85). For all his stress on the importance of religious, philosophical, moral, and cultural factors, and despite his reputation as the "theoretician of the superstructure," Gramsci never denied that the economic mode of production provided the fundamental background against which social and historical change must be analyzed. Gramsci believed that an analysis of the "economic moment" in the process of a social formation is crucial because it allows us "to discover whether in a particular society there exist the necessary and sufficient conditions for its transformation—in other words, to check the degree of realism and practicability of the various ideologies which have been born on its own terrain, on the terrain of the contradictions which it has engendered during the course of its development" (Gramsci 1971: 181). Elsewhere he insists that there can be no cultural reform without economic reform. "Intellectual and moral reform has to be linked with a programme of economic reform—indeed the programme of economic reform is precisely the concrete form in which every intellectual and moral reform presents itself" (Gramsci 1971: 133).[3]

For his part, Weber, no less than Gramsci, also stressed the importance of economic factors for the analysis of social and historical change. He made this quite explicit in his discussion of the rise of Western rationalism.

It is …our first concern to work out and to explain genetically the special peculiarity of Occidental rationalism, and within this field that of the modern Occidental form. Every such attempt at explanation must, recognizing the fundamental importance of the economic factor, above all take account of the economic conditions.

(Weber cited in Bocock 1986: 84)

Comments such as these notwithstanding, however, both Weber and Gramsci also insisted that it was crucial for accounts of change to allow for the influence of ideological and cultural factors, especially religious and moral conceptions of the world, upon human behavior and social action. Thus Weber wrote that "the magical and religious forces, and the ethical ideas of duty based upon them, have in the past always been among the most important formative influences on conduct" (cited in Bocock 1986: 84).

Weber was especially interested in locating historical points of "breakthrough"—roughly equivalent to what Gramsci described as "conjunctural" periods of history. These were periods in the development of a society when circumstances pushed a fundamental social group either toward a new way of action—a "breakthrough"—or toward a reaffirmation of the old way (Gramsci's "passive revolution"). Weber believed that religion had often played a prominent role in these social-historical breakthroughs (McGuire 2008: 248), and, in a famous passage from "The Social Psychology of the World Religions," he wrote that "'very frequently the 'world images' that have been created by 'ideas' have, like switchmen, determined the tracks along which action has been pushed by the dynamic of interest" (Weber 1946: 280, cited in McGuire 2008: 248).

This view of the relationship between ideas and material reality that is captured by the metaphor of ideas as "switchmen" in the course of history, along with this interest in the part played by religious ethics in social–historical "breakthroughs," parallels Gramsci's stress on the importance of the ideological, cultural, and ethical–political forms that have shaped the nature and outcome of revolutionary struggles throughout history and up to the present day.

According to Gramsci, "Every revolution has been preceded by intense activity of criticism, of cultural penetration, and of the permeation of ideas" (Gramsci cited in Counihan 1986: 7). Beliefs, attitudes, and even superstitions and myths are themselves "material" and "real" factors in the process of social change insofar as they are what inspire people towards action and serve as the catalysts in activating "objective contradictions" that are otherwise no more than empty abstractions (Boggs 1976: 37). "To the extent that ideologies are historically necessary they have a validity which is 'psychological'; they 'organize' human masses and create the terrain on which men move, acquire consciousness of their position, struggle, etc." (Gramsci cited in Boggs 1976: 37).

This re-evaluation of the role of ideas and values in social-historical change has led some to raise questions about the nature and extent of Gramsci's Marxism. Some writers have argued that Gramsci was a neo-idealist and quasi-liberal who abandoned the essential tenants of historical materialism. Others have defended his credentials as a Marxist, but have debated endlessly over the issue of exactly what sort of a Marxist he was.[4]

Joseph V. Femia helps to bring the nature of Gramsci's Marxism into sharper focus. Femia argues that one thing is shared in common by those who wish to read Gramsci out of the Marxist tradition as well as by those who try to reconcile his work with the more deterministic versions of that tradition in the belief that such a version is the only one that deserves the name "Marxist." What both camps share is that they fail to comprehend how historical materialism can incorporate a crucial role for ideology or consciousness without losing, in the process, the essential economic core that constitutes its uniqueness. According to Femia, it was Gramsci's achievement to fashion just such a synthesis (Femia 1981: 66).

In support of this claim, Femia outlines four models of the relationship between consciousness or the "ideological superstructure" on the one hand, and the economic–technological base (forces of production) on the other hand (1981: 121). Two of these models can be considered non-Marxist: a) consciousness determines base (the idealist view); and b) consciousness and base interact on an equal basis (the conventional view). The two remaining models can be considered Marxian: c) base determines the form of consciousness (classical, "scientific" Marxism); and d) base determines what forms of consciousness are possible.

Femia contends that Gramsci fits into the fourth category, which he proposes to call "open Marxism." The economic base sets, in a strict manner, the range of possible outcomes, but free political and ideological activity is ultimately decisive in determining which alternative prevails. There is no automatic determination, only the creation of a more or less favorable atmosphere for the diffusion of a new ethos (Femia 1981: 121).[5]

It is interesting to observe in passing that, from this perspective, Weber's methodological approach might also appear to fall within this category of "open" or non-deterministic Marxism. While Weber's work is often and rightly viewed as an attempt to refute the crudely deterministic form of historical materialism that had come to dominate the Marxism of his day, there are in fact, as we have seen, a number of important points at which Weber's perspective actually converges with that of Marx and with that of a latter-day Marxist like Gramsci.[6] To be sure, there are any number of things that sharply distinguish Gramsci's and Weber's positions from one another. Among the most significant of these are the different ethical and political convictions that motivate their inquiries into the history of religions, their very different views of the relationship between "theory" or "science" and political practice, and their sharply contrasting views on the nature and desirability of socialism. Yet the *methodological* similarities between their approaches to religion, ethics, and social change are striking.

Regardless of how one ultimately decides the question of Gramsci's identity and status as a "Marxist" writer, what is important to recognize at this point is that his rejection of determinism provides the theoretical basis for a much more dynamic and open-ended understanding of the role of religion and morality in social and political life than do many alternative approaches.

In the first place, Gramsci's work moves us well beyond the view that religion and morality are passive reflections of underlying social and economic factors and interests. His stress on the reciprocal nature of the relationship between "base" and "superstructure" enables us to view religion and morality as active and dynamic elements in social life, both conditioning and conditioned by social and economic processes. Far from always being subordinate elements within the social process, religious and moral ideas and discourses often play a crucial role in the transformation of society and in transitions from one form of social order to another.

Gramsci also moves us well beyond the standard Marxist conception of religion as the "opium of the people." In contrast to both the Marxist and the functionalist preoccupation with "religions of the status quo," Gramsci's work suggests that religion and morality are not necessarily conservative or reproductive forces in society. While it is crucial to maintain a focus on the legitimating role of religion and morality, it is also important to realize that they can often serve as vehicles for the criticism and transformation of prevailing patterns of influence and power.

Gramsci's work is thus an important resource for efforts to develop "a more subtle and flexible" view of religion and morality in social and political life—a view that enables us to assess "how different religious forms attend the needs of different fractions [*sic*] within a society at different moments in their struggle" (Lincoln 2003: 79). This more dynamic and open-ended conception of the role of religion and morality in social and political life is important for efforts to articulate a critical agenda for the comparative study of religion and ethics, because it opens up a whole range of questions having to do with the relationship between religion, morality, and social change. More specifically, it suggests some important directions for the investigation of alternative discursive strategies that have been and can be employed by religious social movements in struggles to change society.

Religious Ethics and the Discourses of Social Change: Reform, Revolution, Transformation

As a first step toward investigating the role of religious–moral discourses in struggles for social change, it is helpful to recall Bruce Lincoln's distinction between "religions of the status quo" and "religions of resistance" (Lincoln 2003: 77–92). As we saw in the preceding chapter, "religions of the status quo" seek to legitimate the distributions of power, wealth, and prestige within an existing social order. Consisting of a worldview and ethic and of the institutional means for the propagation of this worldview and ethic, religions of the status quo seek to provide a transcendent justification for an existing state of affairs.

> Whatever other tenets may be included in such a religion, I would expect to find present a legitimation of the dominant fractions' right to hold wealth, power, and prestige; an endowment of the social order with a sacral aura, mythic charter, or other transcendent justification; and a valorization of suffering within this world, concomitant with the extended promise of nonmaterial compensations for such suffering.
>
> (Lincoln 2003: 79)

According to Lincoln, "the characteristic goal of the religion of the status quo is ideological hegemony throughout the state or empire in which it is active, and to this end it energetically proselytizes, attempting to disseminate its contents to all segments of society" (Lincoln 2003: 82).[7]

But total hegemony is never possible. Religions of the status quo inevitably fail to persuade all segments of society. There always remain groups who feel alienated from or oppressed by the dominant social party. Among these groups there often arise "religions of resistance"—alternative religious ideologies and institutions, alternative worldviews and ethics. These religions of resistance are rooted in the dissatisfaction and suffering that are experienced by certain social–economic, ethnic, and racial groups within a given social order. Religions of resistance express discontent, hostility, and sometimes outright opposition toward the existing state of affairs (Lincoln 2003: 82).

As Lincoln makes clear, the variety of religions of resistance is nearly endless, and it is impossible to reduce them to a small number of "ideal types" without serious distortion. "They may be ascetic, libertarian, or orgiastic; impassioned, cathartic, or quietistic; utopian or nihilist; esoteric, mystical; militant or pacifist; authoritarian, egalitarian, or anarchist; and so on ad infinitum" (2003: 83). For all their diversity, however, religions of resistance are characterized by a common feature: their refusal to accept the religion of the status quo. This refusal may be partial or total. But in either case, religions of resistance will espouse a set of values that differs in some measure from that of the status quo (2003: 83). When taken seriously, these different values result in different modes of action. Religions of resistance encourage behaviors that deviate in some degree from those encouraged by the religion of the status quo.

> This may result in a more rigidly disciplinarian or ascetic ethical stance, as with the Puritans or such Islamic reformers as the Wahhabiya and Sanusiya, or in a more latitudinarian position verging even upon antinomianism, as with the Brotherhood of the Free Spirit or the "Seven Sages of the Bamboo Grove" during the later Han dynasty. The specifics are of little theoretical consequence. What matters most is that such deviance implies—better yet, enacts—defiance.
>
> (2003: 84)

During periods of relative social and economic stability, such defiance may be tolerated, because it represents only an incidental threat to the dominant social order. But during periods of social and economic crisis, refusal to accept the religion of the status quo often leads to stigmatization or suppression of religions of resistance (2003: 83).

In addition to this basic distinction between religions of the status quo and religions of resistance, I believe it is also possible and necessary to distinguish between "passive" and "active" religions of resistance. Here I depart somewhat from Lincoln's categories. Lincoln distinguishes between religions of the status quo, religions of resistance, and religions of revolution. I find it more helpful to distinguish between passive and active religions of resistance and to treat religions of revolution, along with what might be called "religions of reform," as types within the broader category of active religions of resistance (see Figure 5.1).

What I would call "passive" religions of resistance typically exhibit little desire or effort to change or topple the dominant social order. In contrast to religions of the status quo, passive religions of resistance generally do not proselytize widely beyond their own geographical locus and social milieu. Rather, their primary strategy is one of withdrawal from the larger social order. Their main goal is not so much to achieve hegemony as it is to merely survive and to defend themselves from the ideological domination of the religion of the status quo (Lincoln 2003: 85). To this end they often seek to create a relatively self-contained sub-culture or counter-culture of their own. Within the American context, the most obvious examples of such passive religions of resistance would include groups like the Amish along with some Pentecostal and holiness sects.

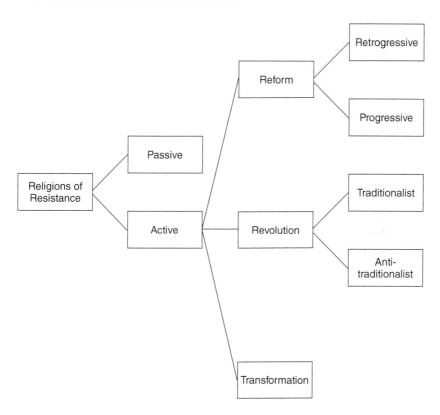

Figure 5.1 Framework for the Analysis of Alternative Discursive Strategies Employed by Religious Social Movements in Struggles for Social Change.

"Active" religions of resistance, on the other hand, do not withdraw from the existing order. Rather, they seek to confront it and to change it. Religious social movements actively seeking to change society will typically adopt one of two general strategies: either reform, or in rare cases, revolution. Reformist and revolutionary strategies for social change are commonly distinguished by focusing on questions about the scale and pace of change and about the degree of violence involved in the process of change. *Reform* is typically more gradual, more narrowly focused on particular problems or sets of issues, and involves less overt violence directed toward persons and property. *Revolution*, on the other hand, is all-encompassing in scope, rapid in tempo, and violent in nature. Revolution is a "total social phenomenon" that not only embraces economic, political, and military issues but religious, cultural, and artistic ones as well (Georges Balandier cited in Lincoln 2003: 91).[8]

But what I wish to stress for purposes of the present discussion is that reform and revolution are distinguished not only by the presence or absence of violence nor by the scale and pace of change. They are also distinguished by the different *discursive strategies*—the different moral languages—that they typically employ. A clarification of the nature and aims of these different discursive strategies and of the concrete projects and interests they represent is one of the main goals of a critical–contextual approach to the comparative study of religion and ethics. Not only can such an inquiry contribute to the growth of "ideological literacy"—the ability to "read" and interpret the political character of religious and moral discourses (Myers 2008: 19)—but it may also contribute to the practical task of social change by expanding our understanding of the various means that can be employed in political struggle.

The language employed by *reform* movements will typically seek to give new meanings to established symbols, ideas, and values. Reformist strategies will try to argue their case within the existing order—its worldview, ethos, and institutional structure—in an effort to change or modify some aspects of that order (Myers 2008: 18). By contrast, the discursive strategy of *revolutionary* movements hinges on the indictment and repudiation of the dominant worldview and ethos altogether. Revolutionary discourse seeks the fundamental redefinition of old terms or the introduction of entirely new ones. Part of what makes revolution such a notoriously complex and difficult project is that it must "simultaneously introduce and legitimate ... new symbols even as it is 'delegitimating' the old ones" (Myers 2008: 19). As Gramsci knew so well, successful revolutionary activity not only involves the criticism and destruction of the old social order, but also "the creation of a novel and original system of moral, juridical, philosophical and artistic relations" (Gramsci 1977: 330).

The *political character* of both reformist and revolutionary strategies for social change is highly ambiguous. On the one hand, a reform movement may seek "retrogressive" change, as in the case of those "fundamentalist" groups around the world who reject secular modernity and who call for a return to the values and lifestyles of a bygone era. The discourse of these conservative reform movements is typically characterized by a nostalgic appeal for a "return to origins" or some prior era. On the other hand, a religious social movement may seek to reform society for the sake of "progressive" change in the sense that it wants to build upon and move beyond present realities. The discourse of progressive reform movements will typically appeal for a fuller realization of the ideological and moral principles and commitments upon which the present social order claims to be based (Myers 2008: 18).

The New Christian Right that emerged in the United States in the 1980s is a good example of a conservative reform movement. Defining itself in opposition to secular humanism, which it views as the religion of the status quo, the Christian Right has self-consciously sought to engage in a "war of myths" (Myers 2008: 14)—a contest about the meaning of America's story and a conflict "over whose symbols shall prevail and who shall have access to symbol selection, definition, and dissemination" (Heinz 1985: 156). One of the Christian Right's primary goals has been to undermine the "liberal establishment's" hegemonic authority and control over such key symbols and institutions in civil society as the family, the schools, and the media. To this end, the movement's discourse has appealed for a return to America's putative Christian identity and heritage in an effort "to rally together the people of this country who still believe in decency, the home, the family, morality, the free enterprise system, and all the great ideals that are the cornerstones of this nation" (Falwell 1987: 245).

The "fractured family" is one of the central symbolic themes in the moral discourse of the religious right. Arguing that "the Bible pattern of family life has been virtually discarded by modern American society" (Falwell 1987: 250), the Christian Right has sought to defend a conception of family life that is based on traditional role expectations for men and women and upon traditional notions of sexual morality. While ignoring the complex economic and social–institutional factors involved, the "pro-family," "pro-life," and "pro-marriage" rhetoric that has figured so prominently in the discourse of this movement has targeted the women's movement and the gay rights movement with much of the blame for the dislocation and breakdown of what it regards as traditional family units. It is in this context that we must understand the Christian Right's moral opposition to abortion rights and to the proposed Equal Rights Amendment to the U.S. Constitution along with its support for the proposed Family Protection Act of 1981 and the Defense of Marriage Act passed in 1996.[9]

In addition to the family, the schools and the media are also important symbols and institutional sites in the Christian Right's counter-hegemonic struggle against modernism and secularism. The Supreme Court's exclusion of school-sponsored prayer and devotional Bible reading from schools was viewed as a direct attack on the Christian Right's myth of America. "It is God Almighty who has made and preserved us as a nation, and the day that we forget that is the day that the United States will become a byword among the nations of the world" (Falwell 1987: 244). Similarly, the effort to have creationism included in the curriculum of public schools and the growth of alternative Christian schools are manifestations of the Christian Right's struggle against what it sees as the hegemony of secular humanism. "The contemporary philosophy that glorifies man as man, apart from God, is the ultimate outgrowth of evolutionary science and secular education" (Falwell 1987: 250).

The media, especially television, has also been an important symbol and site in the struggle for hegemony. Television and radio evangelists and the "electronic church" have been instrumental in bringing the agenda of the Christian Right to the awareness of the wider American public.

> By the end of the 1970s, conservative evangelicals controlled three national television networks, while sixty-six nationally syndicated religious broadcasters, as well as a host of local TV preachers, filled the airwaves with Christian messages. According to Arbitron ratings, 20 million Americans tuned in to watch televangelists, who varied in style from the calm, optimistic Robert Schuller to the shouting and weeping Jimmy Swaggart. Evangelicals had been preaching on radio and television for decades, but televangelism experienced dramatic growth in the 1970s , partly because of the 1960 FCC ruling that allowed stations to use paid religious programs to fulfil their public interest broadcast quotas.
> (Williams 2012: 161)

Convinced that the medium of television is one of the major vehicles by which secular humanism has been implanted in the American mind, the Christian Right's aggressive movement into this medium was designed to propagate a counter-mythology—an alternative worldview and ethos—and must be seen not only as part of a battle for the hearts and minds of the American public, but also as part of a larger struggle for control of the "means of symbolic production" (Heinz 1985: 156).

The family, the schools, and the media all figured prominently in the notorious exchange between Pat Robertson and Jerry Falwell in the aftermath of the 9/11 attacks on the World Trade Center and the Pentagon. In his remarks, Robertson stated that:

> The interests of the people are on their health and their finances, and on their pleasures and on their sexuality, and while this is going on while we're self-absorbed and the churches as well as in the population, we have allowed rampant pornography on the internet. We have allowed rampant secularism and occult, etc. to be broadcast on television. We have permitted somewhere in the neighborhood of 35 to 40 million unborn babies to be slaughtered in our society. We have a court that has essentially stuck its finger in God's eye and said we're going to legislate you out of the schools. We're going to take your commandments from off the courthouse steps in various states. We're not going to let little children

read the commandments of God. We're not going to let the Bible be read, no prayer in our schools. We have insulted God at the highest levels of our government. And, then we say "why does this happen?".

(cited in Lincoln 2003: 104)

Falwell charged that a lot of the blame for the terrorist attacks would have to be shouldered by "the pagans, and the abortionists, and the feminists, and the gays and lesbians who are actively trying to make that an alternative lifestyle, the ACLU, People For the American Way, all of them who have tried to secularize America. I point the finger in their face and say: 'You helped this happen'" (cited in Lincoln 2003: 106).

Not only has the Christian Right contested for influence in the spheres of family life, the schools, and the media, but also in party politics. A common narrative regarding the emergence of the New Christian right is that, after a brief bid for political influence with their anti-evolution campaign in the 1920s, conservative evangelicals and fundamentalists had opted out of politics and retreated to their churches in the aftermath of the Scopes trial. They did not begin to emerge again as a political force until the 1970s when liberal Supreme Court decisions on school prayer, pornography, and abortion provoked them to become politically involved. However, historian Daniel K. Williams has argued that what was new about the New Christian Right of the 1980s was not evangelicals' growing interest in politics, but rather their level of partisan commitment and their increasing influence over the Republican Party (Williams 2012: 1–2).

According to Williams, conservative Protestants had been politically active throughout the twentieth century. In the 1920s they had tried unsuccessfully to mobilize the Democratic Party in defense of Prohibition and had supported the national campaign against evolution led by three-time Democratic presidential candidate William Jennings Bryan. While conservative Protestants came from a variety of denominational backgrounds, they were united in their opposition to evolution, changes in public attitudes toward sexuality and gender roles, and growing Catholic influence in politics, and they shared the belief that America was rapidly losing its Christian moorings and needed to repent. Yet their influence was limited, because neither of the nation's major political parties was receptive to their demands (Williams 2012: 2–3).

The fundamentalist campaigns of the 1920s had failed partly because fundamentalists had not secured control over a political party. Only when conservative Protestants united in support of a comprehensive program that included not only moral legislation, but also economic and foreign policy, could they create the partisan alliance that would give their movement national influence. And conservative Protestants began doing that in the 1940s.

(Williams 2012: 3)

From the 1940s through the 1960s, conservative Protestants began viewing the Republicans as the party of anticommunism and a Protestant-based moral order. Prominent evangelists such as Billy Graham cultivated relationships with President Dwight Eisenhower and Vice-President Richard Nixon, while many self-described fundamentalists supported more conservative Republican leaders such as Strom Thurmond and Barry Goldwater. But their influence over the party was limited by their lack of political skills and by religious divisions within their own movement. By the late 1960s, however, conservative Protestants succeeded not only in making alliances with GOP politicians, but in changing the party's agenda.

> This time they focused more on the culture wars than the Cold War. Conservative Protestants who mobilized against feminism, abortion, pornography, and gay rights acquired control of the Republican Party, partly because of their long-standing alliances with Republican politicians, but perhaps more important because of the united front that they presented, and because of demographic and political shifts that favored evangelicals. By the beginning of the twenty-first century, the Christian Right was the most powerful interest group in the GOP.
>
> (Williams 2012: 3)[10]

The emergence of the New Christian Right in the late twentieth century and its alliance with the Republican Party has not been a passing fad. The Christian Right is many millions strong, and its influence on electoral politics in the U.S. has become increasingly significant since it first helped to sweep Ronald Reagan to the White House in 1980 (Williams 2012: 9).

In contrast to those reform movements whose discourse looks back to a previous era for normative lifestyles and models of social order, it is also possible for religious social movements to seek to reform society for the sake of "progressive change." Arguing that society has failed to live up to its own professed ideals, the discourse of progressive reform movements will typically appeal for a fuller realization of the ideological and moral principles to which the existing order claims to be committed. The early phase of the American Civil Rights Movement, with its appeals to the norms of freedom and opportunity, is perhaps the best example of this approach to social change within recent American history.

During its initial phase, the Civil Rights Movement adopted what Roger D. Hatch has described as a "dilemma" position in the public debate on racial segregation. Its goal was to show that the everyday practice of American life was not in line with the ideals of "liberty," "equality," and "justice for all" that are set forth in the American creed. With its rhetoric and its actions—demonstrations, lawsuits, sit-ins—the movement sought to draw attention to the legal and political impediments that had prevented the full realization of fundamental American values and principles (Hatch 1988a: 162–163).

As one of the leading "organic intellectuals" of the movement, Martin Luther King, Jr. was especially good at casting his criticism of American society and his call for social change in terms that were familiar to the masses of American people. His famous "I Have a Dream" speech, for example, is but one instance in which he is able to draw together the religious and patriotic themes of the American cultural tradition.

> Juxtaposing the poetry of the scriptural prophets—"I have a dream that every valley shall be exalted, every hill and mountain shall be made low"—with the lyrics of patriotic anthems—"This will be the day when all of God's children will be able to sing with new meaning, 'My country 'tis of thee, sweet land of liberty, of thee I sing'"—King's oration reappropriated that classic strand of the American tradition that understands the true meaning of freedom to lie in the affirmation of responsibility for uniting all of the diverse members in society into a just social order. "When we let freedom ring, when we let it ring from every village and hamlet, from every state and every city, we will be able to speed up the day when all of God's children, black men and white men, Jews and Gentiles, Protestants and Catholics, will be able to join hands and sing the words of that old Negro spiritual, 'Free at last! Free at last! Thank God almighty, we are free at last!'" For King, the struggle for freedom became a practice of commitment with a vision of America as a community of memory.
>
> (Bellah et al. 1985: 249)

Similarly, King's discourse in his "Letter from Birmingham Jail" weaves together the biblical and civic republican themes of American civil religion—mentioning Jefferson and Lincoln in the same context as Amos, Paul, and Jesus—in its appeal to more fully realize and fulfil the ideals and principles of the American creed in the everyday life and practice of American society.

King succeeded in doing something that other progressive leaders and reform movements, and especially the American Left, have often been unable or unwilling to do. By casting his criticism of America's past and present and his vision for America's future in terms of the "national–popular" traditions, common sense, and folklore of the American people, he was able to unite disparate groups in a struggle for the intellectual and moral reformation of society.

What is important to observe at this point is that the discourses of both conservative and progressive reform movements share in common an effort to refurbish traditional religious and patriotic symbolism and to assert the authority of a particular definition or interpretation of this symbolism. The reformist strategies of both the New Christian Right and phase one of the American civil rights movement operate on the assumption that the basis of legitimation in American society continues to be a set of values, including notions about God, which were built into the American cultural tradition from the beginning and which have been carried on to the present day by various religious and civic groups. This is also the view that is set forth by

Robert Bellah's conception of American civil religion (Wuthnow et al. 1984: 219; Bellah 1970: 168–190, 1975).

Where these groups differ is on the purpose for which they seek to revitalize traditional symbols—for the sake of retrogressive change in one case, for the sake of progressive change in the other. They also differ in their identification of problems and priorities—compare Falwell's identification of abortion, homosexuality, pornography, secular humanism, and the fractured family as "the five major problems ... that moral Americans need to be ready to face" (1987: 249–250) with King's focus on racism, poverty, and militarism or with Bellah's (1975; Bellah et al., 1985) focus on individualism, consumerism, and American chauvinism. And finally, they differ in their explanations for the causes of these problems—compare Falwell's explanation of social ills in terms of the sinful lifestyles of individuals to King's or Bellah's focus on institutional and social–structural factors.

Just as the religious–moral discourse of reform is politically ambiguous, so also is the *political character of revolutionary discourse*. It may be anti-traditional, as in the classic examples of the French Revolution in 1789 and the Russian Revolution in 1917, or it may be traditionalistic, as in the example of the Iranian Revolution of 1979, which foreshadowed a resurgence of religion's role in geopolitics throughout the late twentieth and early twenty-first centuries.

Modern revolutions are often thought of, almost by definition, as being anti-traditional in their aims and rhetoric. As Roland Robertson has argued (1985: 256), revolutionary discourse since the time of the French Revolution has most often been based on a modern conception of "social problems" (injustice, inequality, lack of freedom) and on the notion that such problems cannot be solved within the outmoded framework that is provided by the exiting religious, moral, and institutional arrangements of society. The solution to such problems therefore requires a revolution, a total overturning of the existing social order and the inauguration of an entirely new form of life.

The Iranian Revolution would appear to be an exception to this pattern of anti-traditionalism. In this case, the rhetoric of traditionalism was employed in an effort to repudiate the "new" order installed by the Shah and his Western allies. The idea here seems to have been that the very ground upon which "modern" social problems had arisen in the first place required a revolution "in order to restore a state of affairs in which the sacred and profane, the material and the ideal, are reunited on the basis of religious doctrine" (Robertson 1985: 255).

While most modern revolutions have been anti-traditional in the sense that they have repudiated existing ideological, moral, and institutional forms, they have not necessarily, for all of that, been anti-religious in their orientation. As we have seen, Gramsci argued that the early stages of the French Revolution should not be interpreted as a repudiation of religion as such, but as a popular struggle to realize the ideals of liberty, fraternity, and equality that were deeply rooted in the popular Christianity of the bourgeoisie and the peasant masses. Moreover, as we have also seen, Gramsci was even willing to view Marxism itself as the inheritor of the revolution that was begun but never completed by primitive Christianity. Similarly, Bruce Lincoln has observed that while many have seen in the English, American, and French revolutions the replacement of a religious theory of legitimacy with a secular theory, this was not the view of the chief actors in these revolutions. On the contrary, the revolutionaries saw such doctrines as the Rights of Man, Popular Sovereignty, and the Social Contract not as less but as more sacred than the Divine Right of Kings.

> For the vast majority of them, the struggle was not one of secular ideology against religion, but of true religion against superstition. One looks in vain for total nonbelievers in the French and English revolutions. As Robespierre, the most fascinating figure of the French Revolution put it: "It is not enough to have overturned the throne; our concern is to erect upon its remains holy Equality and the sacred Rights of man." Nor is his religious language either accident or hyperbole, for it was the Jacobins, led by Robespierre, who sought to establish the cult of the Supreme Being in place of Christianity, and who referred to their messengers as apostles going forth to establish a new religion.
>
> (Lincoln 2003: 87)

Regardless of whether or not the discourse of these modern revolutions was anti-religious, it remains possible to characterize it as anti-traditional insofar as it sought to break the ideological and institutional bounds of the existing society. The distinguishing mark of revolutionary discourse is its effort to repudiate and overthrow the reigning ideals and values and to replace them with an entirely new worldview, ethos, and institutional structure.

A good example of revolutionary discourse in the American context can be found in the Black Power movement of the late 1960s and early 1970s. In contrast to the reformist strategy of the civil rights movement, which sought a more complete realization of American ideals and values, the discourse of Black Power rejected the American creed as bankrupt and as utterly devoid of the resources necessary for solving the problems of racism, poverty, injustice, and oppression. Social change would have to begin and end with a wholesale indictment and repudiation of American ideals, values, and institutions (Hatch 1988a: 164–165).

Malcolm X, the Black Panther Party, and other leaders of the Black Power movement rejected Martin Luther King, Jr.'s call for the construction of a society based on "what was best in the American dream" and on "the most sacred values in our Judaeo-Christian heritage" (King cited in Hatch 1988a: 166). Rather, they argued that the religious and patriotic traditions of America had from the very beginning been tainted and corrupted by the ideology of white supremacy. The problem was not a gap between the American myth and American history, between American ideals and American realities. On the contrary, the problem was that the history and practice of America revealed all too well the true ideals and values upon which it was based (Hatch 1988a: 164–165).

Thus in place of the civil rights movement's focus on *integration* into the mainstream of American life, the Black Power movement promoted *separation* from the corruption of American society as the key to the liberation of African Americans. In place of the civil rights movement's reliance on moral persuasion and non-violence, Black Power was willing to accept the possibility that violence might be a necessary aspect of the struggle for liberation. Indeed, one of the most striking features of the discourse of the movement was its call for the defense and empowerment of black people "by whatever means necessary ... It's either a ballot or the bullet" (Malcolm X 1972: 986, 991).

Although Black Power was united in its repudiation of the American status quo, it was much less unified in its promotion of an alternative vision. While the revolutionary vision of Malcolm X was rooted in religious sensibilities and moral convictions derived from Islam, others such as the Black Panther Party rejected religion and sought to create a black nationalism strongly informed by Third World anti-colonial liberation movements and by the insurrectionary perspectives of such writers as Amilcar Cabral and Frantz Fanon.[11]

Along with this basic distinction between reformist and revolutionary discourses and strategies, I believe it is also possible to identify a third approach—one that provides something of a middle ground between the other two. We can describe this third alternative as a "transformationist" approach to the struggle for social change. Gramsci's work is especially valuable for understanding this third model of the relationship between religious–moral discourses and the struggle to change society.[12]

Here again, it is important to situate Gramsci's perspective within an intellectual and historical context. Since the Bolshevik Revolution of 1917, there had been within Marxism an ongoing debate between two alternative perspectives on the nature of radical social change and on the political strategy most appropriate for its attainment. The revolutionary current within Marxism argued that the effort to bring about fundamental change in society would necessarily have to involve an extralegal and violent insurrectionary struggle that would culminate in the replacement of the bourgeois state by the dictatorship of the proletariat. The advocates of reformism, on the other hand, believed that it was possible to achieve socialism by constitutional means. Through participation in electoral politics it would be possible to win majority control of the government and to use the agency of the state to superintend a peaceful and legal transition to socialism (Coates 1991).

In the polemics between the revolutionary and reformist perspectives, Gramsci always sought to align himself with the revolutionary current within Marxism. He was highly critical of reformism's willingness to accept piecemeal social reforms and its propensity to dilute its radicalism for the sake of gaining momentary electoral advantage. Subsequent history has given little reason to be optimistic about reformism's ability to bring about thoroughgoing social transformation. As David Coates has written:

> Far from proving an effective route to socialism, reformist parties have more normally been the crucial political mechanism through which the working class has been incorporated into a subordinate position within a strengthened bourgeois order (as in England, Norway, Sweden, West Germany and Austria); alternatively, on the rare occasions when they have been more resolute, they have been the harbingers not of socialism, but of the violent suppression of workers by repressive capitalist states (as in Germany in 1933 and Chile forty years later).
>
> (Coates 1991: 461)

Yet, as we have seen, Gramsci also rejected Lenin's insurrectionary model of revolution involving an assault upon the state by a revolutionary vanguard. Rather, he provides the basis for a view of "revolution-as-process," as a long ethical–political struggle, rather than a single political–military event. Gramsci's elaboration of the concept of hegemony as struggle for intellectual and moral leadership within the institutions of civil society and his view of the political party as a vehicle for uniting revolutionary intellectuals and the popular classes within a single democratic institutional framework provides a point of departure for theorizing a "third way" between revolution and reformism as typically understood.

The "transformationist" approach suggested by Gramsci's work is relevant for our effort to understand the alternative discursive strategies that can be employed by religious social movements. It combines *both* the reformist emphasis on the need to draw upon the ideological and moral framework provided by a society's pre-existing religious and patriotic symbols and traditions *and* the revolutionary approach's stress on the need to create new visions and languages that are capable of sustaining the project of a thoroughgoing change in the thinking, practice, and institutional structure of society.

We can perhaps see a concrete example of what a transformationist approach might look like in the American context by considering the discursive strategy that had begun to be employed by Martin Luther King, Jr. near the end of his life in what he called "phase two" of the civil rights struggle. As we have seen, "phase one" of the movement had focused attention on the legal and political spheres of American life. Its goal was to end segregation and to achieve full civil rights for black Americans. In order to achieve these goals, the movement employed a reformist discourse that appealed for the more complete realization of what most U.S. citizens were prepared to recognize as basic American values, namely the values of freedom and opportunity.

After the passage of the Public Accommodations Act in 1964 and the Voting Rights Act in 1965, the movement began to shift its focus of attention from the legal and political spheres to the social and economic spheres of American life. "With Selma and the Voting Rights Act one phase of development in the civil rights revolution came to an end. A new phase opened, but few observers realized it or were prepared for its implications" (King cited in Hatch 1988b: 17).

> When we were in Birmingham we were dealing with the question of the right to have access to public accommodations ... In Selma we were dealing with the question of the right to vote ... Now we are dealing with the problem that is probably the most ... crucial problem of the Negro community, namely, economic deprivation.
>
> (King cited in Sturm 1990: 91)

Thus, while the goal of phase one had been to break down the legal barriers to freedom and opportunity, the goal of phase two would be to empower those who had been prevented from fully participating in American life not only for reasons of racial discrimination, but also for reasons of class and gender discrimination. Along with this change in goals came a shift in discourse from the moral language of civil rights to the language of human rights, from the language of freedom and opportunity to the language of equality and justice (Hatch 1988b: 12–13).

This new phase demanded a new strategy. It would no longer be enough to invoke traditional American symbols and appeal for the more complete realization of traditional American ideals. It would also be necessary to mount a radical critique of key aspects of American thought, practice, policy, and institutions.

> In the days ahead we must not consider it unpatriotic to raise certain basic questions about our national character. We must begin to ask, "Why are there forty million poor people in a nation overflowing with such unbelievable affluence?" Why has our nation placed itself in the position of being God's military agent on earth, and intervened recklessly in Vietnam and the Dominican Republic? Why have we substituted the arrogant undertaking of policing the whole world for the high task of putting our own house in order? ... All these questions remind us that there is need for a radical restructuring of the architecture of American society.
>
> (King cited in Hatch 1988b: 115)

Of course, the gap between rich and poor and the frequency and scale of American military interventions around the world has only grown since 1967, when King wrote these words in his final book, *Where Do We Go From Here: Chaos or Community?*

This increasingly radical critique of the foundations of American society was similar in some respects to the more explicitly revolutionary rhetoric of Black Power. Like the proponents of Black Power, King also viewed the

Civil Rights Movement within the broader global context of Third World liberation struggles against colonialism and imperialism. Already in 1958, King had written that

> This determination of Negro Americans to win freedom from all forms of oppression springs from the same deep longing that motivates oppressed peoples all over the world. The rumblings of discontent in Asia and Africa are expressions of a quest for freedom and human dignity by peoples who have long been the victims of colonialism and imperialism. So in a real sense the racial crisis in America is part of the larger world crisis.
>
> (King cited in Sturm 1990: 92)

There also emerged something of a convergence with Black Power around the idea that radical social change might require more forceful means than moral persuasion and non-violent demonstrations, although King always stopped well short of the Black Power movement's occasional but explicit and well-publicized calls for "retaliatory violence."

> The notion that ethical appeals and persuasion alone will bring about justice [is fallacious]. This does not mean that ethical appeals must not be made. It simply means that those appeals must be undergirded by some form of *constructive coercive power* … Mass nonviolent demonstrations will not be enough … To produce change, people must be organized to work together in units of power. These units may be political … they may be economic.
>
> (King cited in Hatch 1988b: 115, emphasis added)

In contrast to Black Power, however, King's rhetoric never simply negated but also affirmed American culture. "The racism of today is real, but the democratic spirit that has always faced it is also real" (King cited in Hatch 1988a: 166). King never sought the wholesale revolutionary indictment, but rather the wholesale transformation of American society. This could only be achieved through the creation of new visions and languages, new symbols and values in addition to the revitalization of old ones.

> For its very survival's sake, America must re-examine old presuppositions and release itself from many things that for centuries have been held sacred. For the evils of racism, poverty, and militarism to die, a new set of values must be born.
>
> (King cited in Hatch 1988b: 115)

Near the end of his life, King increasingly began to employ the moral language of democratic socialism as a vehicle for articulating these new visions and values, arguing that civil and political rights lack efficacy unless they are accompanied by social and economic rights as well—rights to education, open housing, employment, and a living wage (Sturm 1990: 98).

In order to achieve equality and justice, it would be necessary to confront the triple evils of racism, poverty, and militarism—the structures of oppression upon which modern American society is based. This would require a fundamental restructuring of American society and a "revolution of values."

> For years ... I labored with the idea of reforming the existing institutions of the society ... Now I feel quite differently. I think you've got to have reconstruction of the entire society, a revolution of values.
>
> (King cited in Sturm 1990: 101)

By 1968, however, the coalition that had comprised the civil rights movement had begun to come apart, largely over the issue of equality (Hatch 1988b: 21). King's assassination symbolized, if it did not entirely explain, the disintegration of the movement.

The civil rights movement never really succeeded in completing the transition from the reformist strategy of phase one to the transformationist strategy of phase two, and the goals of phase two—equality, justice, and the democratic empowerment of the poor—all remain unfulfilled to this day. Indeed there is a sense in which the American Civil Rights Movement may be regarded as a classic example of Gramsci's notion of "passive revolution." While it was able to achieve some genuine and significant changes in American life, it was ultimately incorporated into the status quo without substantially altering the structures of power and wealth in American society. This incorporation is symbolized by the official designation of Dr. Martin Luther King, Jr.'s birthday as a national holiday and by the tendency of both the official and popular culture surrounding this holiday to celebrate King as an idealistic dreamer rather than as a radical prophetic critic of the foundations of American society.

Whether or not King might somehow have been able to cast the language of democratic socialism in an American idiom capable of sustaining a collective project aimed at the radical transformation of American ideology and society must forever remain an unanswered question. In this connection it is interesting to note Robert Bellah's response to Frederic Jameson's Marxist critique of *Habits of the Heart*. Bellah claims that "American intellectuals who cannot speak in an American tongue have small audiences, largely confined to the university. If Marxism is ever to be an effective public voice in America, it will have to learn to speak American" (Bellah 1988: 282)

I take this to be precisely Gramsci's point when he insists on the necessity of translating new worldviews, ethics, and programs for social change into the common sense and the "national–popular" traditions of a people. King, along with such all-but-forgotten figures as Eugene V. Debs, are among only a very small handful of progressive leaders in American history who have succeeded in translating their radical proposals into an American idiom that was capable of sustaining, at least for a time, a mass social movement aimed at the intellectual and moral transformation of society.

Conclusion

While the categories I have sketched are oversimplified and stand in need of considerable refinement, I nonetheless believe that they are valuable for generating a series of critical questions that are important for scholarship and teaching in the fields of religious studies and comparative ethics. By asking whether the religious–moral discourses of the traditions that we study are hegemonic or counter-hegemonic; reformist, revolutionary, or transformationist in their strategy; traditionalist or anti-traditionalist in their rhetoric; active or passive, conservative or progressive in character; we can gain a deeper insight into the dynamic nature of religion and morality and into the variety of ways in which religious and moral discourses function in the social and political lives of human communities.

The purpose of such inquiry is not to pigeonhole the moral discourses of particular religious traditions. On the contrary, such an approach requires us to contextualize our analyses so as to recognize the diversity that exists within as well as between all traditions. The discourses of a single religious–moral tradition play a variety of different political roles at different times and in different places. As Ched Myers has written, "the very themes that were liberating in one context can in another become oppressive. The social function of a given ideology cannot be discerned apart from its concrete relationship to the political and economic ordering of power in a determinate formation" (2008: 19).

> Oliver Cromwell, the revolutionary and regicide in England, became Cromwell the oppressor in Ireland (where his name still lives in infamy), and specifically the oppressor of the Catholic peasantry. Dutch protestant burghers could be the heroes of Europe in the Dutch Revolt but villains in Africa with apartheid. The strongly reactionary role of the Catholic church continued in Europe, especially southern Europe, and saw it give active support for Franco in Spain and strike deals with Mussolini and Hitler. It still continues in attenuated form in the main conservative parties in Italy, Spain and southern Germany today. But the countries in Europe where Catholicism and religion in general remained strongest were Ireland and Poland where the church was able, very moderately but powerfully, to identify itself with opposition to national oppression.
> (Molyneux 2008: 21)

What began as a revolutionary worldview and ethic in one time and place can become hegemonic once its proponents have attained power. This is what happened with Christianity after Constantine, with the ideology of bourgeois liberalism after the American and French revolutions, and with

Marxism after the Russian and Chinese revolutions (Myers 2008: 19). Christianity, liberalism, and Marxism all began as counter-hegemonic "religions of resistance" and became "religions of the status quo" serving to legitimate the configurations of power and interest in the new societies that they helped to create. Conversely, once a formerly hegemonic worldview and ethic is displaced, it often becomes a religion of resistance, seeking to mount a counter-hegemonic struggle against those whom it views as having usurped its authority and seeking to restore itself to a hegemonic position in society (Lincoln 2003: 91).

Even after a tradition has become a religion of the status quo, however, it often continues to contain within itself a "subversive memory," which can become the ideological seed of social protest movements (Myers 2008: 19). The prophetic and egalitarian dimensions within Christianity, for example, have regularly inspired movements of social protest ranging from the medieval heresies to the revolt of Anabaptist peasants in the sixteenth century to liberation theology in the late twentieth.

An analysis of the politics of religion and morality, and especially the complex relationship between religious–moral discourses and struggles for social change, should be regarded as an integral part of the comparative study of religion and ethics. Otherwise we will fail to understand fully the dynamic nature and diverse functions of religion and morality in human life.

Notes

1   In his letter to Bloch, Engels wrote that "According to the materialist conception of history, the *ultimately* determining element in history is the production and reproduction of real life. More than this neither Marx nor I have ever asserted. Hence if somebody twists this into saying that the economic element is the *only* determining one, he transforms that proposition into a meaningless, abstract, senseless phrase. The economic situation is the basis, but the various elements of the superstructure— political forms of the class struggle and its results, to wit: constitutions established by the victorious class after a successful battle, etc., juridical forms, and even the reflexes of all these actual struggles in the brains of the participants, political, juristic, philosophical theories, religious views and their further development into systems of dogmas—also exercise their influence upon the course of the historical struggles and in many cases preponderate in determining their *form*" (Marx and Engels 1968: 692).

2   Gramsci illustrates this point with an example taken from the history of Christianity.

> If, for every ideological struggle within the Church one wanted to find an immediate primary explanation in the structure, one would really be caught napping: all sorts of politico-economic romances have been written for this reason. It is evident on the contrary that the majority of these discussions are connected with sectarian and organisational necessities. In the discussion between Rome and Byzantium on the Procession of the Holy Spirit, it would be ridiculous to look in the structure of the European East for the claim that it proceeds only from the Father, and in that of the West for the claim that it proceeds from the Father and the Son. The two Churches, whose existence and whose conflict is dependent on the structure and on the whole of history, pose questions which are principles of distinction and internal cohesion for each side,

but it could have happened that either of the Churches could have argued what in fact was argued by the other. The principle of distinction and conflict would have been upheld all the same, and it is this problem of distinction and conflict that constitutes the historical problem, and not the banner that happened to be hoisted by one side or the other.

(Gramsci 1971: 408–409)

3 In this same connection Gramsci often invoked two basic principles which he derived from Marx and which he believed must orient any discussion of the relationship between base and superstructure "if the forces which are active in the history of a particular period are to be correctly analysed, and the relation between them determined" (1971: 177). The first of these principles is "that no society sets itself tasks for whose accomplishment the necessary and sufficient conditions do not either already exist or are not at least beginning to emerge and develop." The second is "that no society breaks down and can be replaced until it has first developed all the forms of life which are implicit in its internal relations" (1971: 177). Here Gramsci is paraphrasing from memory a passage from Marx's Preface to *A Contribution to the Critique of Political Economy*:

> No social order ever perishes before all the productive forces for which there is room in it have developed; and new, higher relations of production never appear before the material conditions for their existence have matured in the womb of the old society. Therefore mankind always sets itself only such tasks as it can solve; since, looking at the matter more closely, it will always be found that the task itself arises only when the material conditions for its solution already exist or are at least in the process of formation.

(cited by the editors in Gramsci 1971 177)

4 H.S. Hughes (1977: 96–104) comes close to the first position. See Femia (1981: 60–66) and Crehan (2002: 172–176; 199–205) for a summary of some neo-idealist interpretations of Gramsci's position. As for the second position, some writers have insisted that Gramsci was a Leninist, while others have claimed him as the father of the Eurocommunist alternative to Leninism. Some have seen Gramsci as a humanist, while others have sought to reconcile his legacy with Marxism's aspirations to the status of a science (see Althusser and Balibar 1979: 119–144). Still others have seen Gramsci as the inspiration for a movement toward a post-Marxist theory of radical democratic politics that leaves behind the tired polemics about what is and is not genuine Marxism (Laclau and Mouffe 1985). These debates have been aggravated by both the philosophical and the political contexts in which they have taken place. Gramsci's posthumous reputation among the European and American Left is of such a magnitude that disparate factions have sought to lend prestige and legitimacy to their own position by claiming to be the true heirs and guardians of Gramsci's ideas. This has entailed endless arguments about exactly what Gramsci thought, or what he might have thought, about a multitude of topics. See Femia (1979), Jay (1984: 150–173) and Thomas (2010) for a summary of some of these debates.

5 See also Crehan (2002: 88–91) and Eagleton (1976: 1–37) for an illuminating discussion of this issue.

6 See Giddens (1971) and Löwith (1982) for a more extensive discussion of convergences between Weber and Marx.

7 While acknowledging their great differences of detail, Lincoln cites the role of Confucianism in traditional Chinese society, the Church of England under James I and Charles I, and the "selective Christianity" propagated by colonial missions as convenient examples of religions of the status quo (2003: 80–82). In each case "we see an ideology that serves the interests of the dominant fraction, spread by an institution that the dominant fraction supports, and this symbiosis I take to be the hallmark of the religion of the status quo" (2003: 82).

8 See Coates (1991), Kiernan (1991), Markoff (2007), Robertson (1985), and Williams (1983) for a more detailed discussion of the concepts of "reform" and "revolution."

9 In 2013 the U.S. Supreme Court ruled that Section 3 of the Defense of Marriage Act, which restricted U.S. federal interpretation of "marriage" and "spouse" to apply only to heterosexual unions, was unconstitutional under the Fifth Amendment due process clause's guarantee of equal protection (*United States v. Windsor* (570 U.S. __ 2013).

10 Williams' book analyzes these demographic and political shifts, such as the growth of population in the sunbelt and the ascendency of the Republican Party in what had previously been the solidly Democratic southern states, and also provides an account of how the "culture wars" of the 1980s trumped denominational differences between evangelicals and fundamentalists, northerners and southerners, which had long impeded conservative Protestants' political influence.

11 See P. E. Joseph (2009, 2010: 11–34) for insightful accounts of the rhetoric, politics, and history of the Black Power movement and its relationship to the movement for civil rights.

12 The scheme I am seeking to develop here parallels Roger Hatch's analysis of "dilemma," "indictment," and "transformation" as three positions in the public debate on segregation and racism in the United States (1988a). As the present discussion makes clear, I am deeply indebted to Hatch's work. But I have come to this project by a different route than Hatch, and my intention has been to provide a fuller theoretical elaboration of this framework and to extend it in a cross-cultural and comparative direction. It should also be noted that what I am here calling a "transformationist" approach to social change should not be confused with what Gramsci himself knew and criticized as *transformismo* or "transformism" in Italian politics during the era of the Risorgimento. See Gramsci (1971: 58).

6 Religion, Ethics, and Ideology

As a form of critical inquiry, the comparative study of religion and ethics is not only concerned with the question of *how*, but also with the question of *on whose behalf* religions and moralities function. Religious–moral ideas and languages are always those of particular human communities in specific times and places. As such, they are inevitably linked to the interests of particular social groups. This fact presents us with a series of questions about the ideological functions of religion and morality. To what extent are a group's ideas and values merely rationalizations of its own special interests? What role do religious–moral discourses play in struggles for power between dominant and oppositional groups? How are religion and morality involved in the exercise, legitimation, and concealment of domination along lines of class, race, gender, ethnicity, etc.?

While we have touched on these questions in the preceding chapters, in this chapter I will show more specifically how Gramsci's work enables us to maintain a focus on the connection between religious–moral ideas and the interests of social groups while moving beyond the reductionism that has characterized standard Marxist approaches to this issue. I will outline a framework for thinking about the ideological functions of religion and morality and explain how this contributes to our understanding of the critical tasks of religious studies and comparative ethics.

Religious–Moral Discourses and the Interests of Social Groups: The Problem of Reductionism

We have seen that mainstream Marxist theory has regarded both religion and morality as forms of ideology. While the concept of ideology is sometimes ambiguous, its use in this context carries with it a clearly negative connotation. To describe religion and morality as forms of ideology and to characterize religious–moral discourses as "ideological" is to suggest that they embody the vested interests of the dominant groups in society and that they function in such a way as to legitimate the power and privilege of the ruling groups. As Willis Truitt writes, "Morality for Marx and many Marxists is understood to be ideological, i.e., a reflection of the interests of ruling classes and therefore, when accepted and internalized by people who are not members of the ruling class functions as a kind of false consciousness" (2005: vii).[1] From this perspective, religion and morality are elements within "that complex structure of social perception which ensures that the situation in which one social class has power over others is either seen by most of the members of society as 'natural', or not seen at all" (Eagleton 1976: 5).

There are two things to notice about this classic formulation of the Marxist conception of religion and morality as ideology. First, it focuses attention on the relationship between religious–moral discourses and the *material interests* of the dominant group in society. Such material interests—considerations of economic benefits and political power—are what constitute the fundamental basis of social action. Religious, philosophical, and moral discourses are rationalizations of these interests—after-the-fact explanations that justify or mask the real motivations of behavior (McGuire 2008: 238).

The second thing to notice is that this formulation assumes a necessary dichotomy between "sectional interests" and "societal interests." The eventual resolution or transcendence of this dichotomy in favor of the interests of society-as-a-whole awaits the fulfilment of history's progression from feudalism through capitalism to socialism (Giddens 1971: 214). In the meanwhile, any language of universality is simply a form of false consciousness that obscures the conflictual nature of class society. Despite its rhetoric of universal interests and the common good, "morality has always been class morality" (Engels cited in Lukes 1991b: 388).

For all its power to disclose the connections between discourse and interests, this standard Marxist formulation of the problem is overly reductionistic. It fails to take sufficient account of the reality and efficacy of what might well be described as "ideal interests" as distinct from material interests. It also fails to account for the fact that while religious–moral discourses are inevitably linked to the interests of particular social groups in particular times and places, they nonetheless typically amount to more than mere rationalizations of the economic interests of the ruling class.

What makes Gramsci relevant for the present discussion is that his work helps us move beyond the reductionism of the standard Marxist approach while keeping questions about the social location of religion and morality in sharp focus. Gramsci does not deny that the pursuit of interests is the fundamental basis of social action. Nor does he deny that religion and morality often serve to rationalize the interests of the ruling class. There are, however, two major ways in which Gramsci departs from the classic formulation of the Marxist concept of ideology.

First, Gramsci complicates the standard Marxist conception of interests. Implicit in his discussions of religion and morality is a recognition of what Max Weber described as "ideal interests"—interests that are generated by adherence to a set of religious, ethical, or political ideals, values, and principles and which are not identical with nor reducible to underlying material interests (Giddens 1971: 213; Swedberg 2005: 128–131). Appeals to "ideal interests" are a regular feature of practical moral discourses. Whenever one hears the claim that one's "true" interests are more fully served by adhering to one's religious, moral, or political principles rather than by sacrificing those principles for the sake of material gain or political expediency, one is hearing an appeal to "ideal interests."

Ideal interests are not only capable of influencing the actions and lifestyles of individual members of social groups. They can also influence a group's collective perceptions of its own material (economic and political) interests, as, for example, in debates about whether the "true" or "best" interests of the United States are better served by imposing human rights standards on its trading partners or by relaxing such standards for the sake of expanding markets.

Recalling the words of Weber cited in the preceding chapter, "Not ideas, but material and ideal interests, directly govern men's conduct. Yet very frequently the 'world images' that have been created by 'ideas' have, like switchmen, determined the tracks along which action has been pushed by the dynamic of interest" (1946: 280).[2] Weber's classic works on Protestantism and capitalism and on the economic ethics of the world's religions are attempts to demonstrate the power in the "real world" of the "ideal" interests that are generated by religious and moral conceptions of the world.

We have seen that in Gramsci one finds a similar effort to establish the efficacy of religious, ethical, and political ideals and values. At the very heart of the Gramscian conception of hegemony is the notion that social groups are the carriers of worldviews, ethics, and myths—beliefs, values, and stories—that can influence social actions every bit as much as can their own narrow economic interests. For Gramsci as for Weber, ideas and values cannot simply be deduced from the economic interests of groups or classes (Bocock 1986: 88).

Yet even if we are willing to acknowledge that religious–moral discourses may embody ideal as well as material interests, there remains a question about the extent to which such discourses are capable of transcending the *sectional* interests (whether material or ideal) of particular social groups. Here we come to the second way in which Gramsci's work enables us to move beyond the reductionism of the standard Marxist formulation of the concept of ideology.

In the *Manifesto of the Communist Party*, Marx and Engels had written that the "ruling ideas of each age have ever been the ideas of its ruling class" (1968: 51). As Michael Walzer has pointed out, the Gramscian conception of hegemony considerably complicates this basic dictum of Marxism (1988: 447). It does so by affirming that it is both possible and necessary for religious–moral discourses to transcend the narrow self-interest of particular social groups. According to Gramsci, a truly hegemonic class—one that "rules" through intellectual and moral leadership as contrasted with one that simply "dominates" through force and coercion—must be able and willing to go beyond the simple expression and defense of its own narrow economic interests in order to present itself plausibly as the representative of the "universal interests" of disparate groups in society.

Walzer observes that Marx and Engels had actually said something similar in *The German Ideology* when they wrote that "each new class which puts itself in the place of the one ruling before it, is compelled, merely in order to carry through its aim, to represent its interest as the common interest of all the members of society ..." (cited in Walzer 1988: 447). But within the mainstream of the Marxist tradition, the predominant view became that all ruling groups *falsely* represent their own interests as the universal interest of society. In a class-based society, all such talk of universal interests is simply part of "the mechanics of class deception" (Trotsky cited in Lukes 1991b: 388).

Gramsci, on the other hand, indicates that such representation of universal interests is not necessarily and in all cases a mere pretense or form of deception and false consciousness. On the contrary, for Gramsci, the ruling ideas of an epoch are always something more than mere rationalizations of class interest (Walzer 1988: 447). In order to overcome the dichotomy between sectional and societal interests, which is central to the classical Marxist concept of ideology, Gramsci introduced a basic distinction between what he described as "economic–corporate" and "ethical–political" forms of consciousness and discourse. Gramsci borrowed this terminology from the philosophy of Benedetto Croce and used it in an effort to theorize the process by which a social group attains the degree of organization and self-consciousness that is necessary for the successful conquest of political legitimacy.

According to Gramsci, all fundamental social classes (those necessary for the reproduction of a given form of society, for example, the bourgeoisie and the proletariat in industrial capitalism) begin with what he describes as an "economic–corporate" frame of mind or conception of the world. By this Gramsci refers to a stage in the development of a social group when its identity is defined primarily in terms of its own relatively narrow economic interests. In the case of the proletariat, this would be equivalent to the frame of mind that Lenin described as "trade union consciousness" (1961). Correspondingly, the "economic–corporate" outlook of the bourgeoisie might well be described as a form of "possessive individualism" (Macpherson 1962). From either of these perspectives, social and political life is viewed as little more than the direct expression and pursuit of economic self-interest.

In order to achieve a genuinely hegemonic position in society, however, a social group must undergo a "catharsis" in which it passes from an economic–corporate or "egotistic–passional" frame of mind to an "ethical–political" stage of intellectual and moral development (see Gramsci 1971: 366).[3] This is an historical phase in which a particular group moves beyond a position of corporate existence and defense of its own economic position and aspires to a position of leadership in the political and social arena (editors in Gramsci 1971: xiv). As Walter Adamson has explained it, this concept of the "ethical–political" designates a transformation of a group's narrow economic stance into a sense of the collective power of a shared vision of what the future can be, and a mutually shared faith in the group's ability to arrive at that destination (1987/8: 329).

According to Gramsci, the ethical–political or hegemonic stage

> is that in which one becomes aware that one's own corporate interests, in their present and future development, *transcend* the corporate limits of the purely economic class, and can and must become the interests of other subordinate groups too. This is the most purely political phase, and marks the decisive passage from the structure to the sphere of the complex superstructures; it is the phase in which previously germinated ideologies … come into confrontation and conflict, until only one of them, or at least a single combination of them, tends to prevail, to gain the upper hand, to propagate itself throughout society—bringing about not only a unison of economic and political aims, but also intellectual and moral unity, posing all the questions around which the struggle rages not on a corporate but on a "*universal*" plane, and thus creating the hegemony of a fundamental social group over a series of subordinate groups.
>
> (1971: 181–182, emphasis added)

Thus, at the very heart of the concept of hegemony is the notion that ideas— religious and moral conceptions of the world— do not come to "rule" unless and until they are expressed in "ethical–political" terms rather than in narrow "economic–corporate" terms. And what distinguishes "ethical–political" from "economic–corporate" discourses is precisely their degree of universality—their ability to transcend the expression of the narrow sectional interests of particular social–economic classes and to encompass the interests and aspirations that are shared in common by the widest number of disparate groups in society.

Now to be sure, when Gramsci speaks here and elsewhere about the ability of ethical–political discourses to "transcend" the economic interests of particular social groups, he does not mean that it is ever possible to completely sever the link between interests and discourse in any absolute sense. On the contrary, we must always retain an awareness of the importance of the relationship between economic or material interests and the ideas and values espoused by social groups. In this connection Gramsci insists that "though hegemony is ethical–political, it must also be economic, must necessarily be based on the decisive function exercised by the leading group in the decisive nucleus of economic activity" (Gramsci 1971: 161).

Similarly, we can only talk about *degrees* of "universality" that are embodied in particular religious–moral languages, because hegemony is never total or complete. No discourse can ever be fully or perfectly representative or expressive of the aspirations and interests of all the disparate groups in society because of the fundamentally conflictual nature of social and political life.

Nevertheless, what this distinction between "economic–corporate" and "ethical–political" discourses does allow us to do is to view religion, morality, and politics in terms that are not strictly class- or interest-based. Ethical– political discourse serves as an "articulating principle" (Mouffe 1979: 10) that coordinates the interests of the leading group in society with the general interests of subordinate groups (Gramsci 1971: 182). The struggle for and the exercise of hegemony must therefore be conceived as a continuous process of forming and re-forming an equilibrium between the interests of the leading group and those of other groups in society: "equilibria in which the interests of the dominant group prevail, but only up to a certain point, i.e. stopping short of narrowly corporate economic interest" (Gramsci 1971: 182). According to Gramsci, "The fact of hegemony presupposes that one takes into account the interests and tendencies of the groups over which hegemony will be exercised, and it presupposes a certain equilibrium, that is to say that the hegemonic groups will make some sacrifices of a corporate nature" (1971: 161).

On this view, the hegemony of a social group is best understood as a relationship of compromises (Sassoon 1982b: 111). The power of a dominant social group—its use of the state apparatus and its hegemonic authority in the institutions of civil society—is always qualified by the ever-changing relations of political forces and by the compromises that it must constantly make if it is to retain its legitimacy in the eyes of those allied groups whose interests it seeks and claims to represent. The hegemonic status of a social group ultimately depends, then, upon its ability to represent the "universal interests" of the widest possible number of groups in society.

From the point of view of the present discussion, what is most significant about Gramsci's distinction between "economic–corporate" and "ethical–political" forms of consciousness is that it enables us to affirm that *a religious and moral discourse of universality and the common interest remains possible and necessary even within the context of a conflict- and interest-based view of society and politics.* By showing that religious–moral ideas and discourses are not always and only, as such and by definition, the rationalizations of the material and sectional interests of the ruling groups in society, Gramsci's work provides the theoretical basis for moving beyond the reductionism of standard Marxist approaches and for rethinking the ideological functions of religion and morality.

The "Universalization" of Moral Ideas

The perspective that I have been sketching helps us to see how religious–moral ideas that originated as expressions of the sectional interests of a particular social group may, in some cases, prove to be capable of a certain "degree of universalization." We can briefly illustrate this point through a consideration of the origins and development of two conceptions that have figured prominently in the religious, ethical, and political struggles and discourses of the modern world, namely, the concepts of "freedom" and "democracy."

The modern conception of freedom originated as an expression of the sectional interests of the bourgeoisie in its struggle against the economic and political restrictions of feudalism. But since that time, this moral idea has been appropriated by and extended to other social groups in different times and places and has assumed the status of what might well be described as a "universal" human interest.

The concept of freedom has typically been defined as the absence of constraints upon the options open to agents (Lukes 1991a: 172). Within the moral discourse of bourgeois liberalism, these constraints, options, and agents have usually been construed in a relatively narrow fashion. Liberalism has tended to confine its view of the constraints on freedom to deliberate interferences or acts of coercion; it has tended to confine its view of the relevant options to whatever agents in fact conceive or choose; and it has tended to confine its view of agents to a consideration of separate individuals, each of whom is seeking to maximize his or her own self-interest in the marketplace (Lukes 1991a: 172). One of the results of this has been a tendency to equate the notion of human freedom with "free trade," "free competition," and "free contract" between worker and employer. The moral discourse of freedom and liberty has thereby provided one of the most significant ideological legitimations for capitalism (Giddens 1979: 193).

In *The Communist Manifesto*, Marx and Engels sought to expose the limited character of these "bourgeois freedoms." Free trade, free competition, and freedom of contract are in their view not true instances of human freedom at all, because the individuals engaged in such activities (for example, the worker who enters into a contract of employment) are constrained by any number of economic forces that leave them little or no genuine choice in the matter (Norman 1983: 182–183). Marx and the subsequent discourse of socialism drew upon the tradition of Rousseau, Kant, and Hegel in promoting a wider and richer view of freedom as self-determination. On this view, freedom is equated with emancipation from all of those objective and subjective factors that stand as obstacles to the full realization of one's humanity (Lukes 1985, 1991a: 172).

While providing a valuable critical perspective on the moral discourse of liberalism, this broad view of freedom as human emancipation has often led Marxists to dismiss too lightly or even to denigrate the "bourgeois freedoms" (economic and civil liberties) of liberal polities (Giddens 1979: 193; Lukes 1991a: 173). This has been especially true of Marxism–Leninism, which has tended to deny that the formal freedoms of bourgeois democracies have the status of genuine freedoms at all (Lukes 1991a: 173).

What such perspectives have failed to see is that the limited character of bourgeois political and legal freedoms does not make them any the less genuine (Lukes 1984: 147, 1985: 76–80). Indeed, many of these bourgeois freedoms have actually turned out to be capable of a certain degree of universalization: they have been extended to and appropriated by groups other than the bourgeoisie, due in large part to the struggles of the labor movement and the black and women's liberation movements (Giddens 1979: 193). Thus while it is true that "freedom of contract," for example, continues to serve an ideological function by obscuring the true character of relations of production in capitalist societies, it has also at the same time been employed as a tool by the labor movement for facilitating a real extension of the rights of workers (Giddens 1979: 193–194). Similarly, the civil rights and liberties of bourgeois democracies have proven to be indispensable vehicles for the real extension of the rights of women, racial and ethnic minorities, gays, and lesbians.

The extension of the idea of "democracy" provides another example of the universalizing potential of what was originally a sectional ideal (Giddens 1979: 194; Lukes 1984: 84–87). The liberal democracies of the West have rested upon the idea of equality before the law and freedom to form political associations. While these two principles originally served the sectional interests of the entrepreneurial class, their extension helped to make possible the achievement of the mass franchise, something that the dominant classes perceived as a danger to the liberal state until late in the nineteenth and early twentieth centuries (Giddens 1979: 194).

Since that time, the tradition of democratic socialism has sought the further universalization of the idea of democracy by extending it beyond the narrowly political sphere and into the social and economic domains of life. While the discourse of socialism has often degenerated into little more than an expression of the "economic–corporate" or sectional interests of the working class, it is important to remember that neither Marx nor Gramsci endorsed this view. For both Marx and Gramsci, socialism was to be understood not as an expression of the narrow interests of the working class, but as an expression of universal human interests. Both identified the cause of proletarian emancipation with the cause of human emancipation in general, and the future society they envisioned was one in which the interests of all human beings, not just the interests of the proletariat, could be realized (Norman 1983: 186–187). Needless to say, parties claiming to be Marxist have more often than not been extremely undemocratic and oppressive in their policies. However, the gap between moral ideals and social–political realities is not something that is unique to Marxism, and unless one is prepared to argue for the abandonment of all moral ideals that have not been fully realized, a vision of human emancipation and genuine democracy remains relevant in our contemporary world.

This question of the "degrees of universality" exhibited by different religious–moral ideas and discourses has some important implications for our understanding of the critical tasks of the comparative study of religion and ethics. I will return to a brief consideration of these at the conclusion of this chapter.

Rethinking the Ideological Functions of Religion and Morality: Domination and Liberation

By moving beyond the reductionism of standard Marxist approaches, the concept of hegemony and the distinction between "economic–corporate" and "ethical–political" forms of consciousness and discourse set the theoretical context for rethinking the ideological functions of religion and morality. In this new non-reductionistic context, religious–moral discourses appear not only as tools for the legitimation and concealment of domination but also as vehicles for the critique of oppression and the emancipatory transformation of societies.

As Cornel West has explained, Gramsci's reformulation of the standard Marxist concept of ideology presupposes three major points that are important for the analysis of the politics of religion and morality.

> First, it accents the equivocal character of culture and religion, their capacity to be instruments of freedom or domination, vehicles of liberation or pacification. Second, it focuses on the ideological function of culture and religion, the necessity of their being either forces for freedom or domination, liberation or pacification. Third, it views the struggle between these two forces as open-ended. The only guarantee of freedom rests upon the contingencies of human practice; the only assurance of liberation relies on the transformative modalities of a society. No matter how wide the scope of hegemonic culture may be, it never encompasses or exhausts all human practice or every transformative modality in society. Human struggle is always a possibility in any society and culture.
>
> (2002: 120)

In view of the ambiguous ideological functions of religion and morality, a critical–contextual approach to the comparative study of religion and ethics must continue to focus on the role of religious–moral discourses in the legitimation and concealment of *domination* along the lines of class, race, gender, ethnicity, sexual orientation, and so on, but it must also seek to clarify the part that has been and can be played by such discourses in struggles for *liberation* from such domination.

There are two main ways in which religion and morality may be involved in the exercise of domination. One of these, as we have seen, is to represent the sectional interests of ruling groups as the universal interests of society as a whole, thereby legitimating or concealing the patterns of domination upon which a particular social order is based. The liberal bourgeois discourse of human freedom as "free competition" and "freedom of contract" was and is ideological in this sense insofar as it is presented as the application of an eternal and self-evident truth rather than as a product of specific historical conditions and a rationalization of specific economic interests. The function of such a discourse is to legitimate the competition and exploitation in a capitalist economy by morally dignifying it with the title of "freedom" (Norman 1983: 183). The liberal bourgeois discourse of freedom and equality conceals what goes on beneath the surface of the exchange process where "this apparent individual equality and liberty disappear and prove to be inequality and unfreedom" (Marx cited in Larrain 1991: 249). Another obvious example of this can be seen in the widespread representation of male interests as universal human interests—what one writer has called the "masculinist usurpation of universality" (Sheila Ruth cited in MacQueen 1988: 153)—which has served to conceal patterns of gender discrimination.

Besides the representation of sectional interests as universal interests, a second way in which religion and morality may be involved in the exercise of domination is through the "naturalization" or "reification" of culturally and historically contingent social relationships, institutional arrangements, and behavioral patterns (Eagleton 2007: 58–61). The history of religions and philosophies is full of examples where hierarchical and often exploitative relationships between social–economic classes, between genders, and between races and ethnic groups are presented as having the fixed and immutable character of natural laws. These examples range from mythic explanations of the tripartite social structure of ancient Indo-European societies to nineteenth-century biblical justifications of American slavery (see Lincoln 1986; Haynes 2002).

Myth and folklore, in particular, have often served to reinforce the power and privilege of men by equating negative moral characteristics with being female. In this connection Graeme MacQueen has noticed that in the *Motif-Index of Folk Literature*, under the heading "Origin of Mental and Moral Characteristics,"

> there is not a single motif concerned with negative characteristics specific to males, whereas among the motifs dealing with women are the following: "Why women are bad," "Bad women because of head exchanged with the devil," "Bad women combination of nine different animals," "Bad women from transformed hog and goose," "Why women are prattlers," "Why women are roving," "Why women are deceitful," … "Why women never have leisure," "Why women are subservient to men," and "Why man excels woman".
> (MacQueen 1988: 152–153)

MacQueen goes on to consider the extent to which such views of women simply reflect the views of the males of the cultures from which the myths were collected, or whether they reflect the views of the mostly male Western ethnographers and index compilers who have contributed their own biases. In this connection he cites Carol MacCormack, who writes that "if we use comparative ethnographic literature to prove that women are universally devalued, the very ethnographies are products of male bias, and the evidence itself is biased and not valid for the conclusion reached" (MacQueen 1988: 153).

By naturalizing the present, religious–moral discourses obscure the historical and dynamic character of human societies. They thereby serve the position of those groups whose interests are bound up with the preservation of the status quo. Moreover, this naturalization of historically contingent and socially structured relationships is not only a common feature of popular moral discourse, as in the invocation of such axioms as "it's God's will" and "the poor ye shall always have with you" as ways of explaining and justifying disparities in power and wealth and thereby rendering them more tolerable. It is also true of intellectual discourse, as for example in Aristotle's assertion that women and slaves are by nature born to be subordinate and in assertions regarding the natural inferiority of non-white peoples by such modern philosophers as Hume and Kant.

In a footnote to his essay "Of National Characteristics" Hume states that:

> I am apt to suspect the negroes, and in general all the other species of men (for there are four or five different kinds) to be naturally inferior to the whites. There never was a civilized nation of any other complexion than white, nor even any individual eminent either in action or speculation. No ingenious manufactures amongst them, no arts, no sciences ... In Jamaica indeed they talk of one negroe as a man of parts and learning; but 'tis likely he is admired for very slender accomplishments, like a parrot, who speaks a few words plainly.
>
> (cited in West 2002: 62)

Similarly, in his *Observations on the Feeling of the Beautiful and the Sublime*, Kant writes that:

> Mr. Hume challenges anyone to cite a simple example in which a negro has shown talents, and asserts that among the hundreds of thousands of blacks who are transported elsewhere from their countries, although many of them have even been set free, still not a single one was ever found who presented anything great in art or science or any other praiseworthy quality, even though among the whites some continually rise aloft from the lowest rabble, and through superior gifts earn respect in the world. So fundamental is the difference between the two races of man, and it appears to be as great in regard to mental capacities as in color.
>
> (cited in West 2002: 62–63)

Cornel West has argued persuasively that the very "structure of modern discourse" has been rooted in racist assumptions and perspectives (2002: 47–65).

Once again, however, it would be a mistake to view religion and morality solely as tools of the dominant class or group in society. The ideological functions of religion and morality are not limited to the legitimation or concealment of domination. As discussed in chapters four and five, religious–moral discourses can also serve as catalysts for the protests and struggles of subordinate groups as they seek to liberate themselves from structures of poverty, powerlessness, and oppression. Historically, these discourses have often served as vehicles for social criticism and as resources for the creation of alternative moral visions and patterns of social life.

In this connection one thinks of how the biblical tradition has been employed as a vehicle for the denunciation of poverty, injustice, and oppression by such diverse groups and movements as the ancient Hebrew prophets, sixteenth-century Anabaptist peasants in Germany, and contemporary feminist, black, and liberation theologians. One also thinks of various messianic movements and revolutionary episodes such as the Taiping rebellion (1851–1864), the North American Ghost Dance (1890), the Kenyan Mau Mau (1952–1956), and the Cargo Cults of Melanesia in which indigenous traditions were formulated in such a way as to provide a basis for attacks on colonial rule (Lincoln 1985: 4).

Thus, in the words of Norberto Bobbio, an adequate conception of the range of ideological functions performed by religion and morality requires that we no longer view ideology "just as a posthumous justification of a power which has been formed historically by material conditions"; instead, we must follow Gramsci's lead by viewing ideologies "as forces capable of creating a new history and of collaborating in the formation of a new power, rather than to justify a power which has already been established" (1979: 36).

Conclusion

In this chapter I have sought to show that critical inquiry into the ideological functions of religion and morality should not simply be equated with the task of "unmasking" the connections between religious–moral discourses and the interests of social groups. For, as we have seen, the inevitable existence of such a connection does not necessarily imply that the claims to universality typically made by religion and morality are illegitimate or illusory.

On the contrary, religion and morality may also serve as vehicles for the creation and expression of "ideal" and "universal" interests that can generate a sense of collective will and identity. Such ideal and universal interests have the capacity to unite disparate groups into what Gramsci described as "historical blocs"—those complex social, economic, and cultural totalities that coalesce at particular historical junctures and are "cemented" by a distinctive worldview and ethic (see Gramsci 1971: 366, 377, 418). Gramsci thus enables us to recover a dimension that is missing from the standard Marxist approach, namely, an understanding of the role that can be played by religious–moral ideas and discourses in the political struggle to articulate common human interests that are shared by members of disparate social groups.

This framework suggests that one of the main items on the agenda of a critical–contextual approach to the study of religion and ethics should be the task of assessing and comparing the *degrees of universality* that are embodied in the moral discourses of particular religious groups or traditions in specific times and places. To what extent do these discourses reflect or rationalize the narrow sectional or "economic–corporate" interests of a particular social group? To what extent do they succeed in identifying or creating and expressing what might be regarded as "universal human interests" that are shared by disparate groups in a given society or historical epoch? Which discourses and traditions are more and which are less inclusive of the interests of the widest number of human beings, regardless of class, race, gender, ethnicity, sexual orientation, etc.? Exactly what are the discursive means by which alternative moral languages seek to empower or disempower, liberate or constrain individuals and groups? And, more fundamentally still, how, if at all, do different traditions of religious–moral discourse define and employ such concepts or themes as "humanity," "interests," "empowerment," and "liberation" or their analogues?

Questions such as these not only serve to guide comparative inquiry into the ideological functions of religion and morality, they also suggest how the study of religion and ethics might begin to contribute to the practical tasks of criticism and social change. By posing questions about the relationship between religious–moral discourses and the interests of social groups, the comparative study of religion and ethics can help to cultivate the kind of "ideological literacy" that makes possible a critical reading of the many religious–moral–political conflicts and debates that swirl around contemporary domestic and global public policy issues. In this way, the study of religion and ethics can make a modest but important contribution to the critique of domination and to the struggle for more humane, free, and democratic forms of social life.

Notes

1 In the context of Marxist theory, an idea or value is ideological insofar as it serves the interests of the dominant class, not simply because it embodies the vested interest of the group that espouses it. For a comprehensive discussion of Marxist and non-Marxist uses of the concept of ideology see Eagleton (2007).

2 In view of the widespread tendency to counter-pose Weberian and Marxist approaches to the study of religion and morality, it is important to remember that in Weber, no less than in Marx, one finds the conviction that people's actions are explained by their *interests* considered in the context of certain structural conditions (McGuire 2008: 248). Weber does not reject the Marxian stress on the motive power of economic interests in history and society. Rather, he complicates such a view by adding a consideration of the power of "ideal interests." I still find Giddens (1971) to be one of the most illuminating discussions of convergences between Weber and Marx.

3 Gramsci writes that "The term 'catharsis' can be employed to indicate the passage from a purely economic (or egotistic–passional) to the ethico-political moment, that is the superior elaboration of the structure into superstructure in the minds of men" (1971: 366).

References

Adamson, W. 1987/8. "Gramsci and the Politics of Civil Society." *Praxis International* **7** (3/4): 320–339.

Agnew, J. 2005. *Hegemony: The New Shape of Global Power.* Philadelphia: Temple University Press.

Althusser, L. and E. Balibar. 1979. *Reading Capital.* London: Verso.

Antliff, M. 2007. *Avant-Garde Fascism: The Mobilization of Myth, Art, and Culture in France, 1909–1939.* Durham/London: Duke University Press.

Arrighi, G. 1993. "The Three Hegemonies of Historical Capitalism." In *Gramsci, Historical Materialism and International Relations,* S. Gill (ed.), 148–185. Cambridge: Cambridge University Press.

Bammel, E. 1984. "The Revolution Theory from Reimarus to Brandon." In *Jesus and the Politics of His Day,* E. Bammel and C. F. D. Moule (eds.), 11–68. Cambridge: Cambridge University Press.

Bellah, R. N. 1970. *Beyond Belief: Essays on Religion in a Post-Traditional World.* New York: Harper & Row.

Bellah, R. N. 1975. *The Broken Covenant: American Civil Religion in Time of Trial.* New York: The Seabury Press.

Bellah, R. N. 1980. "The Five Religions of Modern Italy." In *Varieties of Civil Religion,* R. N. Bellah and P. E. Hammond (eds.), 86–118. San Francisco: Harper & Row.

Bellah, R. N. 1988. "The Idea of Practices in *Habits*: A Response." In *Community in America: The Challenge of "Habits of the Heart",* C. H. Reynolds and R. V. Norman (eds.), 269–288. Berkeley: University of California Press.

Bellah, R. N. et al. 1985. *Habits of the Heart: Individualism and Commitment in American Life.* Berkeley: University of California Press.

Bird, F. 1981. "Paradigms and Parameters for the Comparative Study of Religious Ethics," *Journal of Religious Ethics* **9** (2): 157–185.

Bird, F. et al. 2016. *The Practices of Global Ethics: Historical Backgrounds, Current Issues, Future Prospects.* Edinburgh: Edinburgh University Press.

Bobbio, N. 1979. "Gramsci and the Conception of Civil Society." In *Gramsci and Marxist Theory,* C. Mouffe (ed.), 21–47. London: Routledge & Kegan Paul.

Bocock, R. 1986. *Hegemony.* New York: Tavistock.

Boer, R. 2009. *Criticism of Heaven: On Marxism and Theology.* Chicago: Haymarket.

Boggs, C. 1976. *Gramsci's Marxism.* London: Pluto Press.

Boggs, C. 2012. *Ecology and Revolution: Global Crisis and the Political Challenge.* New York: Palgrave Macmillan.

Boothman, D. 1995. "General Introduction." In *Antonio Gramsci: Further Selections from the Prison Notebooks*, D. Boothman (ed.), xiii–lxxxvii. Minneapolis: University of Minnesota Press.

Boothman, D. 2011. "The Sources for Gramsci's Concept of Hegemony." In *Rethinking Gramsci*, M. E. Green (ed.), 55–67. London/New York: Routledge.

Borg, C., J. Buttigieg, and P. Mayo (eds.) 2002. *Gramsci and Education*. Lanham: Rowman & Littlefield.

Bottomore, T. 1991. "Economism." In *A Dictionary of Marxist Thought*, second edition, T. Bottomore (ed.), 168–169. Cambridge: Basil Blackwell.

Brown, L. R., 2009. *Plan B 4.0: Mobilizing to Save Civilization*. New York: W. W. Norton.

Bucar, E. M. and A. Stalnaker. 2012. "Introduction: The Third Wave of Comparative Religious Ethics." In *Religious Ethics in a Time of Globalism: Shaping a Third Wave of Comparative Analysis*, E. M. Bucar and A. Stalnaker (eds.), 1–26. New York: Palgrave Macmillan.

Buci-Glucksmann, C. 1982. "Hegemony and Consent." In *Approaches to Gramsci*, A. S. Sassoon (ed.), 116–126. London: Writers & Readers.

Buttigieg, J. A. 2005. "The Contemporary Discourse on Civil Society: A Gramscian Critique." *Boundary 2* **32** (1): 33–52.

Buttigieg, J. A. 2009. "Reading Gramsci Now." In *Perspectives on Gramsci: Politics, Culture and Social Theory*, J. Francese (ed.), 20–32. London/New York: Routledge.

Buttigieg, J. A. 2011. "Notes to the Text." In *Antonio Gramsci: Prison Notebooks*, 3 vols, J. Buttigieg (ed. and trans.), vol. 2, 527–614. New York: Columbia University Press.

Coates, D. 1991. "Reformism." In *A Dictionary of Marxist Thought*, second edition, T. Bottomore (ed.), 460–461. Oxford: Blackwell.

Counihan, C. 1986. "Antonio Gramsci and Social Science." *Dialectical Anthropology* **11** (1): 3–10.

Cox. H. 1999. "The Market as God: Living in the New Dispensation." *The Atlantic*. March. http://www.theatlantic.com/magazine/archive/1999/03/the-market-as-god/306397/ (accessed July 22, 2015).

Cox, R. 1993. "Gramsci, Hegemony and International Relations: An Essay in Method." In *Gramsci, Historical Materialism and International Relations*, S. Gill (ed.), 49–66. Cambridge: Cambridge University Press.

Crehan, K. 2002. *Gramsci, Culture and Anthropology*. Berkeley/Los Angeles: University of California Press.

Croce, B. 1953 [1932]. *History of Europe in the Nineteenth Century*. London: George Allen & Unwin.

Crossley, J. G. 2006. *Why Christianity Happened: A Sociohistorical Account of Christian Origins (26–50 CE)*. Louisville/London: Westminster John Knox.

Dalai Lama. 1999. *Ethics for the New Millennium*. New York: Riverhead.

Daly, H. E. and J. B. Cobb, Jr. 1994. *For the Common Good: Redirecting the Economy Toward Community, the Environment, and a Sustainable Future*, second edition. Boston: Beacon Press.

Day, R. J. F. 2005. *Gramsci is Dead: Anarchist Currents in the Newest Social Movements*. London: Pluto Press.

Durkheim, E. 1965 [1912]. *The Elementary Forms of Religious Life*. New York: Free Press.

Eagleton, T. 1976. *Marxism and Literary Criticism*. Berkeley: University of California Press.

Eagleton, T. 2007. *Ideology: An Introduction*, new and updated edition. London: Verso.

Egan, D. 2008. "Book review: *Power and Resistance in the New World Order* by Stephen Gill; *Paradigm Lost: State Theory Reconsidered*, Stanley Aronowitz and Peter Bratsis, eds." *Review of Radical Political Economics* **40** (2) 252–256. http://rrp.sagepub.com/content/40/2/252 (accessed July 2014).

Elliott, N. 2012. "Diagnosing an Allergic Reaction: The Avoidance of Marx in Pauline Scholarship." *The Bible and Critical Theory* **8** (2): 3–15.

Entwistle, H. 1979. *Antonio Gramsci: Conservative Schooling for Radical Politics*. London: Routledge & Kegan Paul.

Falwell, J. 1987. "A Biblical Plan of Action." In *Border Regions of Faith: An Anthology of Religion and Social Change*, K. Aman (ed.), 244–250. Maryknoll: Orbis.

Femia, J. V. 1975. "Hegemony and Consciousness in the Thought of Antonio Gramsci." *Political Studies* **23** (1): 29–48.

Femia, J. V. 1979. "The Gramsci Phenomenon: Some Reflections." *Political Studies* **27** (3): 427–483.

Femia, J. V. 1981. *Gramsci's Political Thought*. Oxford: Clarendon Press.

Finocchiaro, M. A. 1988. *Gramsci and the History of Dialectical Thought*. Cambridge: Cambridge University Press.

Fiori, G. 1973. *Antonio Gramsci: Life of a Revolutionary*. New York: Schocken.

Fontana, B. 1993. *Hegemony and Power: On the Relation between Gramsci and Machiavelli*. Minneapolis: University of Minnesota Press.

Fontana, B. 2002. "Hegemony and Rhetoric: Political Education in Gramsci." In *Gramsci and Education*, C. Borg, J. Buttigieg, and P. Mayo (eds.), 25–40. Lanham: Rowman & Littlefield.

Forgacs, D. 1984. "National–Popular: Genealogy of a Concept." In *Formations of Nation and People*, B. Schwarz et al. (eds.), 83–98. London: Routledge & Kegan Paul.

Forgacs, D. 1988. "Glossary." In *An Antonio Gramsci Reader: Selected Writings 1916–1935*, D. Forgacs (ed.), 420–431. New York: Schocken.

Francese, J. (ed.). 2009. *Perspectives on Gramsci: Politics, Culture and Social Theory*. New York: Routledge.

Francis. 2015. *Laudato Si' (On Care for Our Common Home)*. Vatican. http://w2.vatican.va/content/francesco/en/encyclicals/documents/papa-francesco_20150524_enciclica-laudato-si.html (accessed August 7, 2015).

Freeden, M. 2003. *Ideology: A Very Short Introduction*. Oxford: Oxford University Press.

Fulton, J. 1987. "Religion and Politics in Gramsci: An Introduction." *Sociological Analysis* **48** (3): 197–216.

Geertz, C. 1973. *The Interpretation of Cultures*. New York: Basic.

Giddens, A. 1971. *Capitalism and Modern Social Theory*. Cambridge: Cambridge University Press.

Giddens, A. 1978. *Emile Durkheim*. New York: Penguin.

Giddens, A. 1979. *Central Problems in Social Theory*. Berkeley: University of California Press.

Gill, S. 2008. *Power and Resistance in the New World Order*, second edition. New York: Palgrave Macmillan.

Gill, S. 2009. "Pessimism of the Intelligence, Optimism of the Will: Reflections on Political Agency in the Age of 'Empire.'" In *Perspectives on Gramsci: Politics, Culture and Social Theory*, J. Francese (ed.), 97–109. New York: Routledge.

Giroux, H. A. 1988. *Teachers as Intellectuals: Toward a Critical Pedagogy of Learning*. New York: Bergin & Garvey.

Gramsci, A. 1971. *Selections from the Prison Notebooks*, Q. Hoare and G. Nowell Smith (eds. and trans.). New York: International Publishers.

Gramsci, A. 1973. *Letters from Prison*, L. Lawner (ed. and trans.). New York: Harper & Row.

Gramsci, A. 1977. *Selected Political Writings*, Q. Hoare (ed. and trans.). New York: International Publishers.

Gramsci, A. 1994. *Pre-Prison Writings*, R. Bellamy (ed.), V. Cox (trans.). New York: Cambridge University Press.

Gramsci, A. 1995. *Further Selections from the Prison Notebooks*, D. Boothman (ed. and trans.). Minneapolis: University of Minnesota Press.

Gramsci, A. 2011. *Prison Notebooks*. 3 vols., J. Buttigieg (ed. and trans.). New York: Columbia University Press.

Green, R. M. 1978. *Religious Reason: The Rational and Moral Basis of Religious Belief.* Oxford: Oxford University Press.

Green, R. M. 1988. *Religion and Moral Reason: A New Method for Comparative Study.* New York: Oxford University Press.

Hatch, R. D. 1988a. "American Racism." In *Issues of Justice: Social Sources and Moral Meanings*, W. R. Copeland and R. D. Hatch (eds.), 153–174. Macon: Mercer University Press.

Hatch, R. D. 1988b. *Beyond Opportunity: Jesse Jackson's Vision for America*. Philadelphia: Fortress Press.

Haynes, S. R. 2002. *Noah's Curse: The Biblical Justification of American Slavery.* Oxford/ New York: Oxford University Press.

Heinz, D. 1985. "Clashing Symbols: The New Christian Right as Countermythology." *Archives de Sciences Sociales des Religions* **59** (1): 153–173.

Hindery, R. 2008. "Comparative Ethics, Ideologies, and Critical Thought." *Journal of Religious Ethics* **36** (2): 215–231.

Howson, R. 2011. "From Ethico-Political Hegemony to Post-Marxism." In *Rethinking Gramsci*, M. E. Green (ed.), 167–176. London and New York: Routledge.

Hughes, H. S. 1977. *Consciousness and Society: The Reorientation of European Social Thought 1890–1930*, revised edition. New York: Vintage.

Jay, M. 1984. *Marxism and Totality*. Berkeley: University of California Press.

Jennings, J. 1991. "Sorel, Georges." In *A Dictionary of Marxist Thought*, second edition, T. Bottomore (ed.), 509. Oxford: Blackwell.

Joll, J. 1977. *Antonio Gramsci*. New York: Penguin.

Jones, N. 1996. "Capitalism." In *The Oxford Encyclopaedia of the Reformation*, H. J. Hillerbrand (ed.), 256–259. Oxford: Oxford University Press.

Joseph, J. 2003. *Social Theory: Conflict, Cohesion and Consent*. Edinburgh: Edinburgh University Press.

Joseph, P. E. 2009. "The Black Power Movement: A State of the Field." *The Journal of American History* **96** (3): 751–776.

Joseph, P. E. 2010. *Dark Days, Bright Nights: From Black Power to Barack Obama*. New York: Basic Civitas.

Kertzer, D. I. 1979. "Gramsci's Concept of Hegemony: The Italian Church—Communist Struggle." *Dialectical Anthropology* **4** (4): 321–328.

Kiernan, V. G. 1991. "Revolution." In *A Dictionary of Marxist Thought*, second edition, T. Bottomore (ed.), 476–480. Oxford: Blackwell.

Knitter, P. F. and C. Muzaffar (eds.). 2002. *Subverting Greed: Religious Perspectives on the Global Economy*. Maryknoll: Orbis.

Kolakowski, L. 2005. *Main Currents of Marxism*, P. S. Falla (trans.). New York/London: W.W. Norton.

Küng, H. and K.-J. Kuschel (eds.). 1995. *A Global Ethic: The Declaration of the Parliament of the World's Religions*. New York: Continuum.

Kurtenbach, E. 2014. "Annual UN Human Development Report Finds Halting Progress in Key Measures." http://www.usnews.com/news/business/articles/2014/07/24/un-human-development-report-faults-inequality (accessed July 27, 2015).

Laclau, E. and C. Mouffe. 1985. *Hegemony and Socialist Strategy*. London: Verso Press.

Larrain, J. 1979. *The Concept of Ideology*. Athens: University of Georgia Press.

Larrain, J. 1991. "Ideology." In *A Dictionary of Marxist Thought*, second edition, T. Bottomore (ed.), 247–252. Oxford: Blackwell.

Lease, G. 2000. "Ideology." In *Guide to the Study of Religion*, W. Braun and R. T. McCutcheon (eds.), 438–447. London: Cassell.

Lenin, V. I. 1961 [1902]. "What Is To Be Done?" In *Collected Works*, volume 5. Moscow: Foreign Languages Publishing House, http://www.marxists.org/archive/lenin/works/1901/witbd/ (accessed August 2012).

Liguori, G. 2009. "Common Sense in Gramsci." In *Perspectives on Gramsci: Politics, Culture and Social Theory*, J. Francese (ed.), 122–133. London/New York: Routledge.

Lincoln, B. 1985. "Introduction." In *Religion, Rebellion, Revolution*, B. Lincoln (ed.), 3–11. New York: St. Martin's Press.

Lincoln, B. 1986. *Myth, Cosmos, and Society: Indo-European Themes of Creation and Destruction*. Cambridge: Harvard University Press.

Lincoln, B. 2003. *Holy Terrors: Thinking about Religion after September 11*. Chicago: University of Chicago Press.

Lincoln, B. 2012. *Gods and Demons, Priests and Scholars: Critical Explorations in the History of Religions*. Chicago: University of Chicago Press.

Little, D. and S. Twiss. 1978. *Comparative Religious Ethics: A New Method*. New York: Harper & Row.

Longenecker, B. W. 2009. "Socio-Economic Profiling of the First Urban Christians." In *After the First Urban Christians: The Social–Scientific Study of Pauline Christianity Twenty-Five Years Later*, T. D. Still and D. G. Horrell (eds.), 36–59. London/New York: T&T Clark.

Lovin, R. and F. Reynolds (eds.). 1985. *Cosmogony and Ethical Order: New Studies in Comparative Ethics*. Chicago: University of Chicago Press.

Löwith, K. 1982. *Max Weber and Karl Marx*. London: Allen & Unwin.

Loy, D. 1997. "The Religion of the Market." *Journal of the American Academy of Religion* **65** (2): 275–290.

Lukes, S. 1984. *Individualism*. Oxford: Basil Blackwell.

Lukes, S. 1985. *Marxism and Morality*. Oxford: Clarendon Press.

Lukes, S. 1991a. "Emancipation." In *A Dictionary of Marxist Thought*, second edition, T. Bottomore (ed.), 172–173. Oxford: Blackwell.

Lukes, S. 1991b. "Morals." In *A Dictionary of Marxist Thought*, second edition, T. Bottomore (ed.), 387–389. Oxford: Blackwell.

Macpherson, C. B. 1962. *The Political Theory of Possessive Individualism: Hobbes to Locke*. Oxford: Clarendon Press.

MacQueen, G. 1988. "*Whose* Sacred History? Reflections on Myth and Dominance." *Studies in Religion/Sciences Religieuses* **17** (2): 143–157.

Maduro, O. 1977. "New Marxist Approaches to the Relative Autonomy of Religion." *Sociological Analysis* **39** (4): 359–367.

Malcolm X. 1972. "The Ballot or the Bullet." In *The Voice of Black America: Major Speeches by Negroes in the United States 1797–1971*, P. S. Foner (ed.), 985–1001. New York: Simon & Schuster.

Mansueto, A. 1988. "Religion, Solidarity and Class Struggle: Marx, Durkheim and Gramsci on the Religion Question." *Social Compass* **35** (2): 261–277.

Markoff, J. 2007. "Revolution." In *Encyclopedia of Globalization*, R. Robertson and J. Aart Scholte (eds.), 1032–1035. New York: Routledge.

Marx, K. and F. Engels. 1968. *Selected Works*. New York: International Publishers.

Marx, K. and F. Engels. 1975. *Collected Works*, vol. 3 (1843–1844). New York: International Publishers.

Marx, K, and F. Engels. 1976. *Collected Works*, vol. 5 (1845–1847). New York: International Publishers.

McGuire, M. B. 2008. *Religion: The Social Context*, fifth edition. Long Grove: Waveland Press.

McLellan, D. 1987. *Marxism and Religion*. New York: Harper & Row.

McLellan, D. 1995. *Ideology*, second edition. Minneapolis: University of Minnesota Press.

McLellan, D. 2007. *Marxism after Marx*, fourth edition. New York: Palgrave Macmillan.

McNally, M. 2009. "Gramsci's Internationalism, the National–Popular and the Alternative Globalisation Movement." In *Gramsci and Global Politics: Hegemony and Resistance*, M. McNally and J. Schwarzmantel (eds.), 58–75. New York: Routledge.

McNally, M. and J. Schwarzmantel (eds.). 2009. *Gramsci and Global Politics: Hegemony and Resistance*. New York: Routledge.

Molyneux, J. 2008. "More than Opium: Marxism and Religion." *International Socialism*, June 24. http://www.isj.org.uk/?id=456 (accessed July 2012).

Morton, A. D. 2003. "Historicizing Gramsci: Situating Ideas in and Beyond Their Context." *Review of International Political Economy* **10** (1) 118–146.

Mouffe, C. 1979. "Introduction: Gramsci Today." In *Gramsci and Marxist Theory*, C. Mouffe (ed.), 1–18. London: Routledge & Kegan Paul.

Myers, C. 2008. *Binding the Strong Man: A Political Reading of Mark's Story of Jesus*, twentieth anniversary edition. Maryknoll: Orbis.

Nelson, R. H. 2001. *Economics as Religion: From Samuelson to Chicago and Beyond*. University Park: Penn State Press.

Nelson, R. H. 2010. *The New Holy Wars: Economic Religion vs. Environmental Religion in Contemporary America*. University Park: Penn State Press.

Nisbet, R. 1973. *The Social Philosophers: Community and Conflict in Western Thought*. New York: Thomas Y. Crowell.

Norman, R. 1983. *The Moral Philosophers: An Introduction to Ethics*. Oxford: Clarendon Press.

Norman, R. 1998. *The Moral Philosophers: An Introduction to Ethics*, second edition. Oxford: Oxford University Press.

Portelli, H. 1974. *Gramsci et la Question Religieuse*. Paris: Editions Anthropos.

Rampell, C. 2008. "Alternatives to the G.D.P." *New York Times* Economix Blogs October 30, http://economix.blogs.nytimes.com/2008/10/30/alternatives-to-the-gdp/ (accessed July 28, 2015).

Redefining Progress. n.d. "Genuine Progress Indicator." http://rprogress.org/sustainability_indicators/genuine_progress_indicator.htm (accessed June 2016).

Reed, J.-P. 2012. "Theorist of Subaltern Subjectivity: Antonio Gramsci, Popular Beliefs, Political Passion, and Reciprocal Learning." *Critical Sociology* March 14 http://crs.sagepub.com/content/early/2012/03/08/0896920512437391 (accessed December 2012).

Rees, W. E. 2011. "Toward a Sustainable World Economy." http://whatcom.wsu.edu/carbonmasters/documents/TowardSustainableWorldEconomy.pdf (accessed July 27, 2014).

Rees, W. E. 2014. "Avoiding Collapse: An Agenda for Sustainable Degrowth and Relocalizing the Economy." https://www.policyalternatives.ca/publications/reports/avoiding-collapse (accessed July 27, 2015).

Reynolds, F. 1979. "Four Modes of Theravada Action." *Journal of Religious Ethics* **7** (1): 12–26.

Robertson, R. 1985. "The Development and Implications of the Classical Sociological Perspective on Religion and Revolution." In *Religion, Rebellion, and Revolution*, B. Lincoln (ed.), 236–265. New York: St. Martin's Press.

Robinson, W. I. 2014. *Global Capitalism and the Crisis of Humanity*. New York: Cambridge University Press.

Rudé, G. 1980. *Ideology and Popular Protest*. New York: Pantheon.

Salamini, L. 1974. "Gramsci and the Marxist Sociology of Knowledge: An Analysis of Hegemony–Ideology–Knowledge." *The Sociological Quarterly* **15** (3): 359–380.

Santucci, A. A. 2010. *Antonio Gramsci*. New York: Monthly Review Press.

Sassoon, A. S. 1982a. "A Gramsci Dictionary." In *Approaches to Gramsci*, A. S. Sassoon (ed.), 12–17. London: Writers & Readers.

Sassoon, A. S. 1982b. "Hegemony, War of Position and Political Intervention." In *Approaches to Gramsci*, A. S. Sassoon (ed.), 94–115. London: Writers & Readers.

Sassoon, A. S. 1982c. "Editor's Notes." In *Approaches to Gramsci*, A. S. Sassoon (ed.), 116–117. London: Writers & Readers.

Schwarzmantel, J. 2009a. "Introduction: Gramsci in His Time and in Ours," In *Gramsci and Global Politics: Hegemony and Resistance*, M. McNally and J. Schwarzmantel (eds.), 1–16. New York: Routledge.

Schwarzmantel, J. 2009b. "Gramsci and the Problem of Political Agency." In *Gramsci and Global Politics: Hegemony and Resistance*, M. McNally and J. Schwarzmantel (eds.), 79–92. New York: Routledge.

Shafir, G. 2002. "Interpretive Sociology and the Philosophy of Praxis: Comparing Max Weber and Antonio Gramsci." In *Antonio Gramsci: Critical Assessments of Leading Political Philosophers*, J. Martin (ed.), vol. 2, 49–61. London: Routledge.

Smart, N. 1983. "Conclusion." In *Religion and Politics in the Modern World*, P. H. Merkl and N. Smart (eds.), 267–273. New York: New York University Press.

Sorel, G. 1950 [1908]. *Reflections on Violence*. New York: Collier.

Stanley, J. L. 1981. *The Sociology of Virtue: The Political and Social Theories of Georges Sorel*. Berkeley: University of California Press.

Stanley, J. L. 2002. *Mainlining Marx*. New Brunswick/London: Transaction.

Steger, M. B. 2009a. *Globalisms: The Great Ideological Struggle of the Twenty-First Century*, third edition. Lanham: Rowman & Littlefield.

Steger, M. B. 2009b. *Globalization: A Very Short Introduction*. Oxford: Oxford University Press.

Sturm, D. 1990. "Martin Luther King, Jr. as Democratic Socialist." *Journal of Religious Ethics* **18** (2): 79–105.

Swedberg, R. 2005. *The Max Weber Dictionary: Key Words and Central Concepts*. Stanford: Stanford University Press.

Texier, J. 1979. "Gramsci, Theoretician of the Superstructures." In *Gramsci and Marxist Theory*, C. Mouffe (ed.), 48–79. London: Routledge & Kegan Paul.

Thomas, P. D. 2010. *The Gramscian Moment: Philosophy, Hegemony and Marxism*. Chicago: Haymarket.

Tonkin, J. 1996a. "Marxism." In *The Oxford Encyclopaedia of the Reformation*, H. J. Hillerbrand (ed.), 25–28. Oxford: Oxford University Press.

Tonkin, J. 1996b. "Reformation Studies." In *The Oxford Encyclopaedia of the Reformation*, H. J. Hillerbrand (ed.), 398–410. Oxford: Oxford University Press.

Truitt, W. H. 2005. *Marxist Ethics: A Short Exposition*. New York: International.

Twiss, S. B. 2005. "Comparison in Religious Ethics." In *The Blackwell Companion to Religious Ethics*, W. Schweiker (ed.), 147–155. Malden: Blackwell.

UNHDR. 2014. "United Nations Human Development Report 2014—Sustaining Human Progress: Reducing Vulnerabilities and Building Resilience." http://hdr.undp.org/en/content/human-development-report-2014 (accessed July 29, 2015).

U.S. Department of Defense. 2014. *Climate Change Adaptation Roadmap* http://www.defense.gov/Releases/Release.aspx?ReleaseID=16976 (accessed July 29, 2015).

Wainwright, J. 2010. "On Gramsci's 'Conceptions of the World.'" *Transactions of the Institute of British Geographers* **35** (4): 507–521.

Walsh, W. H. 1969. *Hegelian Ethics*. London: Macmillan.

Walzer, M. 1988. "The Ambiguous Legacy of Antonio Gramsci." *Dissent* **35** (4): 444–456.

Watkins, E. 2011. "Gramscian Politics and Capitalist Common Sense." In *Rethinking Gramsci*, M. E. Green (ed.), 105–111. London/New York: Routledge.

Weber, M. 1946. *From Max Weber: Essays in Sociology*, H. H. Gerth and C. W. Mills (eds. and trans.). New York: Oxford University Press.

West, C. 2002. *Prophesy Deliverance! An Afro-American Revolutionary Christianity*, anniversary edition with a new preface by the author. Louisville: Westminster John Knox Press.

Williams, D. K. 2012. *God's Own Party: The Making of the Christian Right*. Oxford/New York: Oxford University Press.

Williams, R. 1978. *Marxism and Literature*. Oxford: Oxford University Press.

Williams, R. 1981. *Culture*. Glasgow: Fontana.

Williams, R. 1983. *Keywords: A Vocabulary of Culture and Society*, revised edition. New York: Oxford University Press.

World Council of Churches. 2003. "Lead Us Not Into Temptation: Churches' Response to the Policies of International Financial Institutions." https://www.oikoumene.org/en/resources/documents/wcc-programmes/public-witness-addressing-power-affirming-peace/poverty-wealth-and-ecology/neoliberal-paradigm/lead-us-not-into-temptation (accessed August 7, 2015).

World Social Forum. 2006. http://www.wsfindia.org/ (accessed July 28, 2015).

Wuthnow, R. et al. 1984. *Cultural Analysis: The Work of Peter L. Berger, Mary Douglas, Michel Foucault and Jürgen Habermas*. Boston: Routledge & Kegan Paul.

Index